The BASEBALL FANBOOK

Gary Gramling

Design by Beth Bugler

Indians shortstop Francisco Lindor made sure some fans went home with souvenirs.

Writer: Gary Gramling
Designer: Beth Bugler
Editor: Elizabeth McGarr McCue
Copy Editor: Pamela Roberts
Reporter: Jeremy Fuchs
Illustrator: Colin Hayes
Production Manager: Hillary Leary

ISBN: 978-1-68330-069-4
Library of Congress Control Number: 2017959536

First edition, 2018

1 QGV 18

10 9 8 7 6 5 4 3 2 1

We welcome your comments and suggestions about
Time Inc. Books. Please write to us at:

Time Inc. Books
Attention: Book Editors
P.O. Box 62310
Tampa, FL 33662-2310
(800) 765-6400

timeincbooks.com

Time Inc. Books products may be purchased for business or
promotional use. For information on bulk purchases, please
contact Christi Crowley in the Special Sales Department
at (845) 895-9858.

CONTENTS

INTRODUCTION **6**

Chapter **1**

KNOW THESE NUMBERS
A list of records—some breakable, some
untouchable—that you need to have down pat **8**

Chapter **2**

OBSCURE FACTS
Some of the coolest noteworthy baseball nuggets **38**

Chapter **3**

SKILLS TO MASTER
Learn how to do things the right way—even eat
sunflower seeds **68**

Chapter **4**

RUN A TEAM
Assemble your roster, then survive the longest season in
pro sports. This is how MLB franchises are built **86**

Chapter **5**

HE REMINDS ME OF . . .
Which stars of today play like the stars of yesteryear? **98**

Chapter **6**

TEAM TIDBITS
Find out a little something about each of the 30 MLB teams **128**

Chapter **7**

TALK THE TALK
If you want to be a real baseball fan, you have
to know the lingo **164**

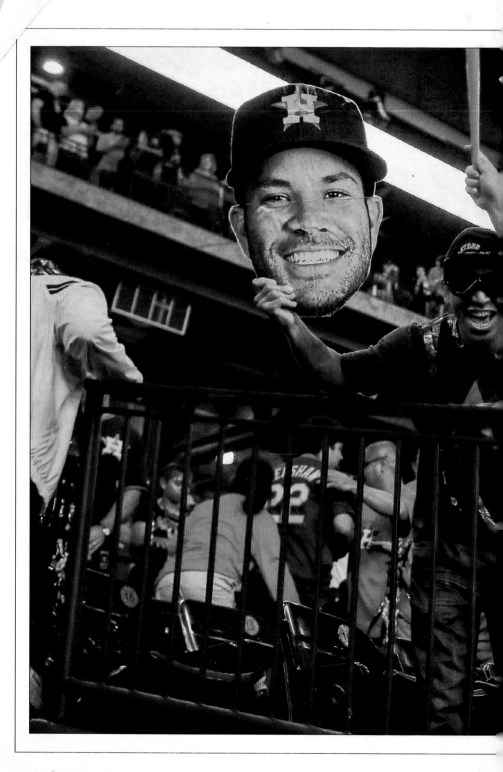

Houston fans were pretty pumped a certain magazine predicted correctly that José Altuve and the Astros would win the 2017 World Series.

Introduction

T here is nothing in the world like attending a baseball game. There's the way it looks—the contrast between the deep green of the manicured grass, the light brown infield dirt, and the gleaming white bases and foul lines. There are the smells (hot dogs, if you're lucky). And there are the sounds: the sudden *crack* of the bat or *pop* of the ball hitting the catcher's mitt.

Most team sports are similar: One squad tries to take the ball to the other team's side of the field or court and put it into a goal. In baseball, the defense decides when play begins. Then it's 1 on 9, the hitter trying to get the ball to land where the nine opponents can't catch it.

enhancing drugs. In the end, we decided not to. There were players linked to steroids who were not likable people (such as Barry Bonds). There were some who were linked to PEDs but got more of a pass because they were so popular (such as David Ortiz). And there are surely dozens who simply didn't get caught.

The game's earlier days weren't perfect either. A gambling scandal tarnished the 1919 World Series, and African-American players were kept out of the major leagues until 1947. But it's impossible to tell the story of baseball without everyone who has been part of the game.

And history is crucial to understanding baseball. The game hasn't undergone the radical changes that other sports in America have. Unlike football and basketball, the sport you watch today is relatively similar to the one your parents and your grandparents enjoyed. When I was a kid, my family and I bonded over Baltimore Orioles baseball. (We still do!) And when my kids are a little bit older, they can join in too. I hope this book will help dads, moms, grandmas, grandpas, and every superfan in between share the game they love with the kids they love.

I love baseball because it is unique. That doesn't mean it's perfect, though. Pitching changes take too long, umpires' strike zones are inconsistent, and man, it gets hot at summer afternoon games. There are bigger problems too. During my lifetime, there was the sportwide scandal of the steroids era. In this book, we considered simply cutting out any mention of a player who had been linked to performance-

Gary Gramling

KNOW THESE NUMBERS

True students of the game must have important statistics at their fingertips. We've gathered a list of records—some breakable, some untouchable—that you need to have down pat.

CAREER HOME RUN LEADERS

762 Barry Bonds
(1986–2007)

755 Hank Aaron
(1954–1976)

Who is MLB's home run king? For many, the answer is simple: the guy who hit the most home runs. That's Bonds, the slugger for the Pirates and the Giants who dominated baseball like no one since Babe Ruth. A dark cloud hung over Bonds's power display, however, because of suspected steroid use. He had grown noticeably larger late in his career and went from averaging a home run every 17.4 at bats in his 20s to every 10.3 at bats in his 30s, including his historic 73-homer season in 2001.

Hammerin' Hank had power and unusual longevity: He had eight 40-home-run seasons, the first at age 23, the last at 39. He socked home run number 715 in 1974, nearly 39 years after Babe Ruth had hit his 714th—and final—career homer. Aaron received death threats while on his record run because of a combination of Ruth's legend and the color of Aaron's skin. Because Aaron's home runs came before the steroid era of the 1990s and 2000s, many still recognize him as the home run king.

??? Josh Gibson
(1930–1946)

868 Sadaharu Oh
(1959–1980)

Or was the real home run king not even allowed to play in the majors? MLB was segregated until 1947, forcing Gibson to play in the Negro leagues instead. Known as the Black Babe Ruth, Gibson has a Hall of Fame plaque saying that he hit "almost 800 home runs" over 17 seasons in various independent leagues. The total could have been more—the slugging catcher was just 35 and still playing when he died in January 1947 after suffering a stroke.

If we're talking about the worldwide home run king, that title clearly belongs to Oh. The greatest to ever play in Japan's Nippon Professional Baseball, Oh obliterated the ball over his 22 seasons with the Yomiuri Giants, though the competition in Japan is a half-step below what it is in the U.S. He hit 55 home runs in 1964 to set Japan's single-season record, a mark that stood until Curaçaoan-born former MLB player Wladimir Balentien hit 57 in 2013.

60 Babe Ruth

New York Yankees, 1927

Ruth was so dominant that he changed the way baseball was played. When he slugged 29 home runs for the Red Sox in 1919, it was a single-season record. A year later, after joining the Yankees, he nearly doubled the mark, hitting 54. His 60-homer season stood as the record until 1961 and is the most ever hit in a 154-game season.

61 Roger Maris

New York Yankees, 1961

Maris was challenging two legends in the summer of 1961. There was, of course, Babe Ruth, the record holder at the time. And there was Mickey Mantle, Maris's teammate and the most famous player in baseball, who was also chasing Ruth's record. (Mantle would end up with 54.) Maris's mark had an asterisk next to it since he played a 162-game season and Ruth had only played 154.

73 Barry Bonds

San Francisco Giants, 2001

Mark McGwire had baseball's first 70-home-run season, reaching that mark in 1998. Bonds hit his 70th with three games to go in the 2001 season, then followed it up with two home runs the next day (plus one more in the season finale). Because of their alleged steroid use, many feel Bonds's and McGwire's marks should carry an asterisk as well.

MOST CAREER GRAND SLAMS

25

Alex Rodriguez

(1994–2013, 2015–2016)

Rodriguez is another player from baseball's steroid era whose feats will never be considered legitimate by many. (Rodriguez admitted to using performance-enhancing drugs for a three-year period, from 2001 through 2003.) Among those feats were a whopping 25 career grand slams; those helped him become one of three 20th-century players (with Hank Aaron and Babe Ruth) to amass 2,000 career RBIs (2,086).

MOST HOME RUNS IN A SINGLE GAME

4   18 PLAYERS

Since 1894, 18 players have slugged four home runs in a game, including five future Hall of Famers: Ed Delahanty (1896), Lou Gehrig (1932), Chuck Klein (1936), Willie Mays (1961), and Mike Schmidt (1976). In 2017 two players accomplished it during the same season for the second time. On June 6, Scooter Gennett of the Reds did it in a 13–1 win over the Cardinals, and on September 4, J.D. Martinez *(above)* of the Diamondbacks did it in a 13–0 win over the Dodgers with two solo shots and two two-run homers.

MOST CAREER HOME RUNS ALLOWED

522

Jamie Moyer

(1986–1991, 1993–2010, 2012)

Moyer pitched for a long time—25 seasons, until he was 49—and most of his career was during the homer-happy days of the 1990s and 2000s. That's how he became a different kind of home run king, serving up more four-baggers than any pitcher in big league history.

MOST CAREER HITS

4,256

Pete Rose
(1963–1986)

To be a career leader in just about any category, you don't just have to be great—you have to be great for a long time. That was Rose, who played 24 major league seasons, including one as a player-manager at age 45. Along the way, the tenacious competitor known as Charlie Hustle won three batting titles, led the National League in hits seven times, and amassed 200 or more hits in a season 10 times.

SINGLE-SEASON HITS RECORD

262

Ichiro Suzuki

Seattle Mariners, 2004

The first Japanese position player to find stardom in the U.S., Ichiro had 200 hits in each of his first 10 seasons, including a record 262 in his fourth year. If you include the 1,278 hits he had in Japan, he'd have more career hits than Pete Rose.

MOST HITS IN ONE GAME

9

Johnny Burnett

Cleveland Indians, July 10, 1932

Burnett had a career-high 152 hits in 1932, and a chunk of them came on a record-setting day against the Philadelphia Athletics. Burnett slapped seven singles and two doubles in a game that went 18 innings. For a nine-inning game, the record is seven hits, shared by Wilbert Robinson of the Orioles (June 10, 1892) and Rennie Stennett of the Pirates (September 16, 1975).

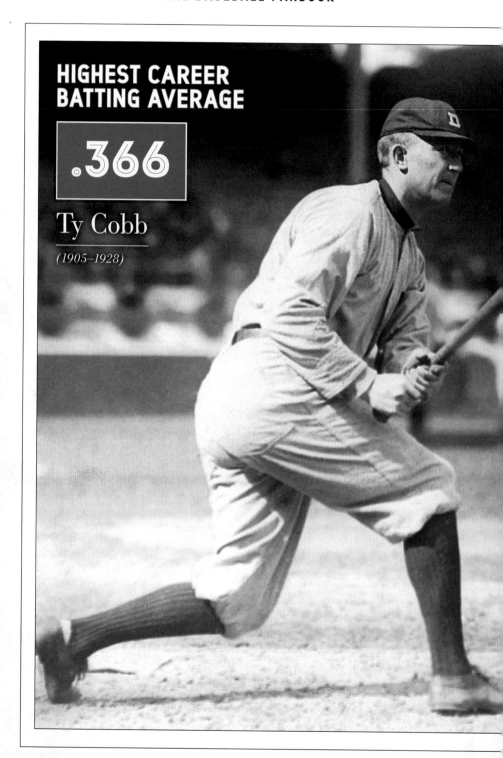

HIGHEST CAREER
BATTING AVERAGE

.366

Ty Cobb

(1905–1928)

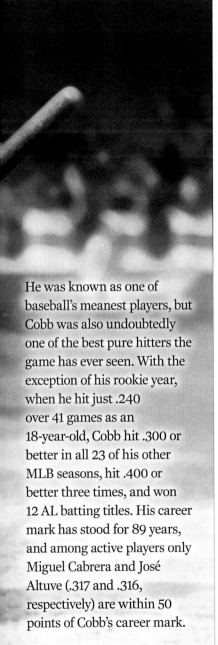

He was known as one of baseball's meanest players, but Cobb was also undoubtedly one of the best pure hitters the game has ever seen. With the exception of his rookie year, when he hit just .240 over 41 games as an 18-year-old, Cobb hit .300 or better in all 23 of his other MLB seasons, hit .400 or better three times, and won 12 AL batting titles. His career mark has stood for 89 years, and among active players only Miguel Cabrera and José Altuve (.317 and .316, respectively) are within 50 points of Cobb's career mark.

HIGHEST SINGLE-SEASON BATTING AVERAGE

.440

Hugh Duffy

Boston Beaneaters, 1894

Duffy broke .400 for the only time in his career in 1894, earning a second straight National League batting title. He wasn't just a singles hitter, either: Duffy led the NL with 18 home runs and 51 doubles that year. Twenty players have ended their seasons with an average of .400 or better (28 times), but no one has done it since 1941.

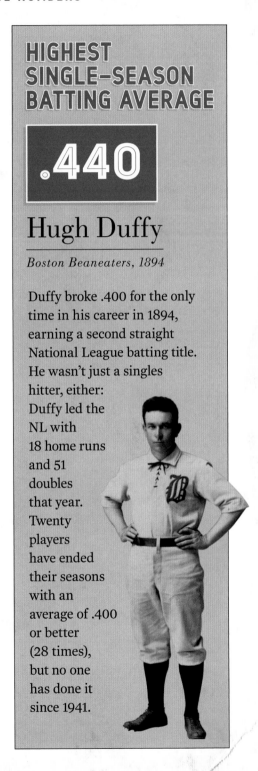

LONGEST HITTING STREAK

56

Joe DiMaggio

New York Yankees,
May 15–July 16, 1941

George Sisler's record of getting a hit in 41 consecutive games had stood for nearly two decades before Joltin' Joe went on his run. DiMaggio often said he wasn't thinking about the record as the streak extended, but by the time it was over, he had blown it away. In fact, the day he snapped it, Indians third baseman Ken Keltner made two sparkling defensive plays to rob DiMaggio of hits. The Yankees' star then went on to hit safely in 16 straight games after that, so if not for Keltner's defensive gems, DiMaggio's streak might have been 73!

MOST CONSECUTIVE GAMES PLAYED

2,632

Cal Ripken Jr.

Baltimore Orioles,
May 30, 1982–September 19, 1998

During May of his rookie season in 1982, Ripken sat out the second game of a doubleheader. After that, he was in the starting lineup for nearly 17 seasons' worth of Orioles games. On September 6, 1998, the night he broke Lou Gehrig's record by playing in his 2,131st straight game, the action was delayed for 22 minutes after the top of the fifth inning (when it became an official game). Ripken received a standing ovation as he jogged around the ballpark high-fiving fans.

MOST CONSECUTIVE GAMES WITH A HOME RUN

8 TIE

Ken Griffey Jr.

*Seattle Mariners,
July 20–28, 1993*

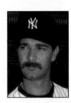

Don Mattingly

*New York Yankees,
July 8–18, 1987*

Dale Long

*Pittsburgh Pirates,
May 19–28, 1956*

Only 21 players in big league history have hit at least one home run in six consecutive games (Barry Bonds did it twice), and just six have stretched the streak to seven. These three are the only ones who have gone deep in eight straight games. Mattingly actually hit 10 home runs while on his eight-game streak, swatting two in a game twice during his spree. Those accounted for one-third of his home run output in 1987.

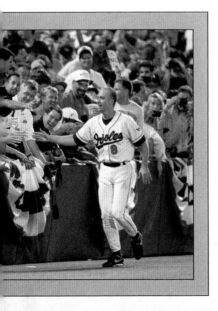

LOWEST SINGLE–SEASON ERA (LIVE BALL)

1.12

Bob Gibson

St. Louis Cardinals, 1968

How phenomenal was Gibson in 1968? After the season, Major League Baseball lowered the height of the pitching mound (from 15 inches to 10 inches) and shrunk the strike zone to give hitters a better chance. Pitchers around the league dominated in 1968, but no one performed like Gibson, who won the NL Cy Young Award and league MVP. He threw 13 shutouts over 34 starts. Amazingly, he lost nine games that season, as the Cardinals' offense scored only 3.03 runs per game for him.

LOWEST SINGLE–SEASON ERA (DEAD BALL)

0.86

Tim Keefe

Troy Trojans, 1880

Dead Ball era or not, Keefe's 1880 season was historically stellar. It ranks as the best ever in terms of the advanced statistic Adjusted ERA+, which factors in home ballpark and the league's average ERA.

MOST WINS

511

AND LOSSES

316

BY A PITCHER

Cy Young

(1890–1911)

It probably won't surprise you that the pitcher who had more wins and losses in baseball history also started more games in the big leagues (815) than anyone else. Of course, Young didn't just pitch for a long time—he was *outstanding* for a long time. He led the AL and the NL in ERA once each and led his league in wins five times.

MOST SINGLE-SEASON WINS BY A PITCHER

59 | Old Hoss Radbourn

Providence Grays, 1884

Radbourn started 73 games that season and also won the NL's pitching crown by leading the league in ERA (1.38) and strikeouts (441).

MOST CAREER SHUTOUTS

110

Walter Johnson

(1907–1927)

Johnson, known as the Big Train, was a unique—and uniquely dominant—pitcher. The righty's fastball was once clocked at more than 91 mph, a velocity few pitchers could match in the early 20th century. But unlike many hard throwers, he had a sidearm delivery, making it even tougher for righthanded batters to hit against him. Along with having thrown the most shutouts, Johnson is one of only two pitchers to win 400 career games (417) and was baseball's all-time strikeout leader for more than 50 years (3,509).

MOST CAREER SAVES

Mariano Rivera
(1995–2013)

652

As a minor leaguer in the 1990s, Rivera was often better known for being the cousin of the Yankees' top prospect at the time, Ruben Rivera, than a budding star in his own right. Mariano, in fact, became a star quite by accident. He discovered his devastating cut fastball while playing catch before a game during his first season as the Yankees' closer, when he and a teammate couldn't figure out why every one of his throws kept darting at the last minute. Over the next 17 seasons, that cutter would establish Rivera as the greatest closer ever.

MOST SINGLE–SEASON SAVES

62

Francisco Rodriguez
Los Angeles Angels, 2008

Sometimes it takes a little bit of luck to rack up saves. That was the case for Rodriguez, a dominant reliever who wasn't at his best in 2008. He blew seven saves in what was arguably the worst of his seven seasons with the Angels. L.A. won enough close games, however, that K-Rod finished as the only man to ever save 60 in a season.

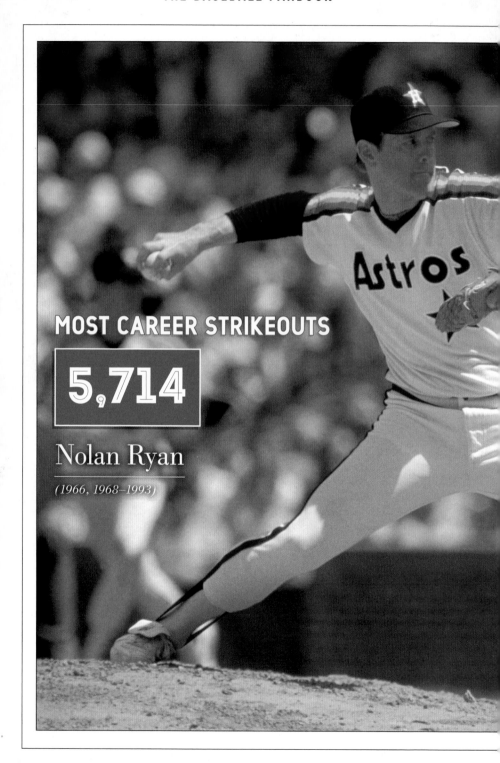

MOST CAREER STRIKEOUTS

5,714

Nolan Ryan

(1966, 1968–1993)

His fastball regularly hit 100 mph, and he was also a little wild, making batters shake in their cleats as they stood in to face down the Ryan Express. For 27 seasons Ryan was one of baseball's best pitchers. His strikeout record was about much more than simply pitching for a long time, though. Of the 134 pitchers in baseball history to throw 3,000 or more innings in their careers, only Ryan and Randy Johnson averaged more than a strikeout per inning.

Ryan's Impressive Records

27
SEASONS
Spanned seven presidential administrations

7
CAREER NO-HITTERS
No one else has thrown more than four

383
STRIKEOUTS IN A SEASON
A Live Ball era record

MOST CHAMPIONSHIPS

27 New York Yankees

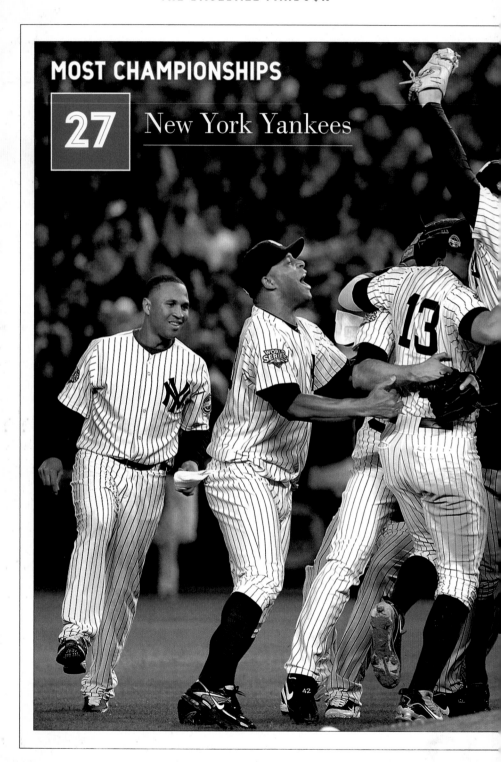

The Yankees have always had a bit of an advantage over the rest of baseball. They are one of the game's wealthiest franchises, so they have been able to afford players many other teams can't. Still, you have to win the games, and the Yanks boast some pretty impressive dynasties. They won 10 World Series in 21 seasons between 1923 and 1943. They won six in seven years from 1947 to 1953. And, most recently, they won four titles in five years from 1996 to 2000, including a three-peat from 1998 to 2000 (especially impressive in the wild-card era, when teams have to win three series to get their rings). The Yankees have more championships than anyone across the major professional sports. Only the NHL's Montreal Canadiens (24), the Premier League's Manchester United (20), and the NBA's Boston Celtics (17) even come close.

MOST WORLD SERIES CHAMPIONSHIPS BY A PLAYER

Yogi Berra

(1946–1963, 1965)

As mentioned on the previous page, the Yankees have won more titles than any team in baseball history. And one of their most beloved stars, Berra, has won more titles than any individual player, one ring for every finger. Berra was considered the leader of the outstanding Yankees dynasty that ran through the 1950s and won five straight World Series titles between 1949 and 1953. In his 17 full seasons with the Yankees (starting in 1947), Berra played in the Series in all but three of those years. He wasn't just along for the ride, either. He was named AL MVP three times (1951, 1954, 1955) and made 18 All-Star appearances (two All-Star Games were played in four of those seasons, from 1959 through 1962).

MOST REGULAR-SEASON WINS

116 TIE

Chicago Cubs
_1906_

Seattle Mariners
_2001_

The best regular-season teams of all time enjoyed some bittersweet success: Despite all those wins, they fell short in October. The 1906 Cubs own the highest winning percentage (.763) of any team post-1900 but lost that year's World Series to their crosstown rivals, the White Sox. The Mariners tied the Cubs' win record nearly a century later but couldn't get past the Yankees in the 2001 American League Championship Series, losing in five games.

MOST STRIKEOUTS IN A GAME BY A PITCHER

20

Roger Clemens
Boston Red Sox, April 29, 1986
Boston Red Sox, September 18, 1996

Kerry Wood
Chicago Cubs, May 6, 1998

Max Scherzer
Washington Nationals, May 11, 2016

ROGER CLEMENS

MOST CAREER RBIs

2,297

Hank Aaron

(1954–1976)

No one in baseball history drove in more runs than Hammerin' Hank, who had 100 RBIs in 11 of his 22 full big league seasons and led

MOST RBIs IN A SEASON

191

Hack Wilson

Chicago Cubs, 1930

How good was Wilson in 1930? He was still picking up RBIs nearly 70 years later. He was thought to have finished the 1930 season with a record 190 RBIs, but in 1999 baseball historian Jerome Holtzman discovered that one of Wilson's RBIs had accidentally been credited to a teammate. Since 1940, no one has come within even 25 RBIs of Wilson's mark.

the National League in the category four times. A lot of it had to do with the fact that, while his home run totals are often his most recognized achievement, Aaron was far more than just a power hitter. He won two NL batting titles early in his career and retired with a .305 lifetime batting average.

MOST CAREER RUNS SCORED

2,295 Rickey Henderson

(1979–2003)

If you want to score a lot of runs, it helps if you're fast. But more than anything, you have to get on base a lot. Along with being a quality hitter (he hit .300 in a season eight times), Henderson drew a lot of walks. Thanks to a good eye (and an exaggerated crouch at the plate, which made his strike zone smaller), he was one of four players in history to have more than 2,000 walks in his career. Henderson led the AL in walks four times, leading to a career .401 on-base percentage, and led the league in runs five times.

MOST CAREER STOLEN BASES

1,406 Rickey Henderson

And Rickey could really run. He's the only player to ever steal more than 1,000 bases. He also holds the modern-era record for steals in a season (130 in 1982); Hugh Nicol recorded 138 in 1894, but back then players were credited with a steal if they took an extra base on a hit (for instance, going from first to third on a single).

MOST CAREER STRIKEOUTS

2,597

Reggie Jackson

(1967–1986)

Sometimes even the great ones strike out. A lot. Jackson was one of baseball's best at the plate, slugging 563 career homers and earning the nickname Mr. October for his World Series heroics. However, he actually finished his career with more strikeouts than hits.

MOST STRIKEOUTS IN A SEASON

223

Mark Reynolds

Arizona Diamondbacks, 2009

Advanced statistics proved over the years that strikeouts, while bad, aren't quite as devastating as managers and players used to think they were. In fact, players who draw a bunch of walks also strike out a lot because they patiently wait for their pitches. Enter Reynolds, who hit 44 homers with 102 RBIs and had a solid .349 on-base percentage in 2009. He also managed to go down on strikes more than anyone ever had in a season, his second of three straight 200-K years!

FASTEST PITCH

105.1 MPH

Aroldis Chapman

Cincinnati Reds,
September 24, 2010
New York Yankees
July 18, 2016

Clocking a pitch's velocity has been an inexact science over the years. But according to data tracked by PITCHf/x technology, used since 2007, no one has thrown a pitch faster than Chapman. His heater hit 105.1 mph against Tony Gwynn Jr. of the San Diego Padres in 2010. (Gwynn took the pitch for a ball, though he eventually struck out after facing a few more 100-plus-mph fastballs.) Chapman matched the velocity six years later against J.J. Hardy of the Orioles.

Chapter

2

OBSCURE FACTS

Did you know that a
major leaguer once got a hit
for two different teams on the
same day? Or that a player
once bonked the same fan twice
in one at bat? Read on for
those and many more
noteworthy nuggets.

MIRROR, MIRROR **PAT VENDITTE WAS MAJOR LEAGUE BASEBALL'S MOST RECENT SWITCH PITCHER.**

It's tougher for a hitter to pick up the ball against a pitcher throwing from the same side (a righty facing a righty, or lefty facing a lefty). That's why Venditte was an unusual weapon during his brief MLB career. He could pitch as a righty against righthanders and as a lefty against lefthanders, the latest of the rare breed of "switch pitchers."

NO. 1 NO ONES **TWO PLAYERS SELECTED FIRST OVERALL IN THE MLB DRAFT NEVER PLAYED IN THE MAJORS.**

The top pick of the MLB amateur draft doesn't always become a star. But since the draft started in 1965, only two No. 1 picks failed to make it to the big leagues. Catcher Steve Chilcott *(top)* was taken first by the Mets in 1966 (the Kansas City A's took Reggie Jackson at No. 2), but a shoulder injury derailed his career. The Yankees selected lefty fireballer Brien Taylor *(bottom)* with the top pick of the 1991 draft, but Taylor injured his pitching shoulder in a fight two years later and never made it to the Bronx.

FANCY **BASEBALL'S FIRST UMPIRES WORE COATS WITH TAILS AND TOP HATS.**

It's no surprise that baseball fashion has changed drastically since the sport's early days, but the most shocking example might be the umpires' duds. When the sport was just starting to gain popularity in the mid-19th century, umpires (frequently local lawyers or doctors, men who were already respected authority figures) were often decked out in formal attire: top hats and jackets with long tails.

YOU'VE GOT MAIL

HANK AARON RECEIVED A PLAQUE FROM THE POST OFFICE FOR RECEIVING TONS OF MAIL.

As he approached Babe Ruth's career home run record in the early 1970s, Aaron received close to a million pieces of mail. The U.S. Post Office recognized him for receiving more correspondence than any American who wasn't a politician.

STRENGTH IN NUMBERS

THE YANKEES HAVE RETIRED MORE NUMBERS THAN ANY TEAM IN BASEBALL.

The club has retired 21 numbers to honor 23 different players, including every number from 1 through 9. Derek Jeter *(right)*, whose number was retired in 2017, had the last single-digit number in use.

LEFTY IN THE 19TH CENTURY MOST BASEBALL DIAMONDS WERE BUILT SO THAT THE BATTER FACED AWAY FROM THE SETTING SUN.

That meant home plate was on the western-most point of the diamond, with second base on the eastern-most point. That's also why lefthanded pitchers became known as "southpaws"—when facing home plate, a lefty's pitching arm was on the south side of the field.

SWITCH HITTER

JOEL YOUNGBLOOD GOT A HIT FOR TWO DIFFERENT TEAMS IN TWO DIFFERENT CITIES ON THE SAME DAY.

On August 4, 1982, Youngblood batted third for the Mets and drove in two runs with a third-inning single against the Cubs at Wrigley Field in Chicago. Then he was pulled from the game because he had been traded to the Expos. Youngblood boarded a flight to Philadelphia, where the Expos were playing that night, entered the game in the bottom of the sixth, and stroked a single in the top of the seventh.

SPACE-SAVER JOURNALISTS TURNED "SOCKS" INTO "SOX."

In the early days of professional baseball, teams' names often had to do with their uniforms. The AL's Chicago team was known as the White Stockings, which took up too much space for newspaper headline writers. The name was often replaced by "Sox," a word that was preferred by linguists who wanted to simplify the English language and differentiate U.S. English from British English. The White Stockings became the White Sox in 1904, and the Boston Americans changed their name to the Red Sox after the 1907 season.

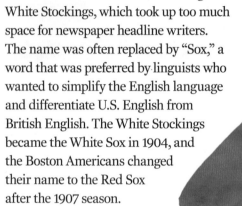

STILL GOT IT BARTOLO COLÓN HIT HIS FIRST HOME RUN AT AGE 42.

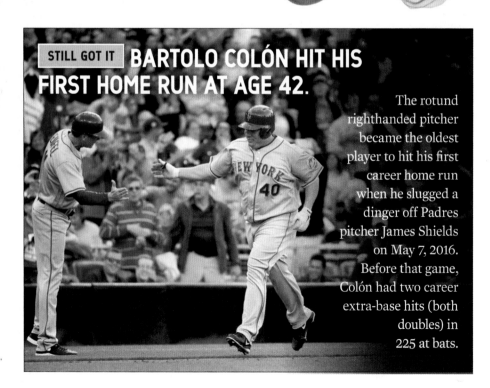

The rotund righthanded pitcher became the oldest player to hit his first career home run when he slugged a dinger off Padres pitcher James Shields on May 7, 2016. Before that game, Colón had two career extra-base hits (both doubles) in 225 at bats.

NOT SUITABLE **THERE'S NO OFFICIAL RULE THAT SAYS A TEAM'S MANAGER MUST WEAR A UNIFORM.**

Perhaps you've wondered why baseball managers wear uniforms, while coaches in every other professional sport do not. Well, it's not an official rule. Many early managers were also players, which created a tradition. Hall of Fame manager Connie Mack *(right),* who retired in 1950 after a 53-season career as an MLB skipper, was one of the last managers to wear street clothes on the bench.

HARD BALL

IN THE MID–19TH CENTURY, BASEBALLS WERE MADE BY THE PLAYERS THEMSELVES.

Often, pitchers fashioned the balls out of whatever materials they could get their hands on. The rubber core was frequently made from pieces of melted shoes, then wrapped in yarn and a leather cover. (Sometimes fish eyes were used for the core. *Whaaaaaaat?*)

MUDDY IT UP.

Before all major league and minor league games, umpires and team staffers rub game balls with a thin coating of special mud to make them easier for pitchers to grip. The mud is all provided by the same company, Lena Blackburne Baseball Rubbing Mud, which gets the muck from an area on the New Jersey side of the Delaware River.

ALL MLB BASEBALLS ARE MADE IN COSTA RICA.

The balls are made by hand by the approximately 300 sewers employed by Rawlings. The company makes 2.4 million baseballs a year and sends around 1.8 million of them to MLB.

APPROXIMATELY 10 DOZEN BALLS ARE USED DURING A NINE-INNING MLB GAME.

Of course, fans can keep balls that go into the stands. That includes home runs, foul balls, and balls given to fans by players. Umpires rotate balls out over the course of a game, and pitchers sometimes request a new ball if they think the one they have is too scuffed up or they don't like the feel of it. Teams also go through close to 200 balls during batting practice.

EVERY BASEBALL HAS 108 STITCHES.

Using exactly 88 inches of waxed red thread, the balls are sewn so that the first and last stitches are hidden. The inside of a baseball consists of wool and yarn, rubber casing, and a cork center.

FAKING IT THE WRITERS OF "TAKE ME OUT TO THE BALL GAME" HAD NEVER BEEN TO A BALL GAME.

Indeed, when Jack Norworth and Albert Von Tilzer wrote the song in 1908, neither had ever actually seen a matchup in person. Norworth's lyrics are about a woman named Katie who agrees to a date as long as the couple goes to a baseball game. The original version was sung by Norworth's wife, Nora Bayes. The song is traditionally played during the seventh-inning stretch at games of all levels, though only the chorus is played. Von Tilzer attended his first game 20 years after the song was released. Norworth attended *his* first game 12 years after that.

SHARING IS CARING IT WAS ONCE COMMON FOR PLAYERS TO LEAVE THEIR GLOVES AT THEIR POSITIONS WHILE THEY BATTED.

Some players shared gloves, while others simply left their equipment on the field while their team was on offense. A rule prohibiting the practice was introduced in 1953.

THE YOUNGEST PLAYER TO APPEAR IN AN MLB GAME WAS 15.

In 1944 the Reds, like many teams, were running short on players because of World War II. So they turned to whiz kid Joe Nuxhall, who had signed a contract the previous winter. Nuxhall (above, *right*) was 15 years, 316 days old when he made his debut on June 10, 1944. He didn't last a full inning—and was sent to the minors afterward—but he returned to the majors in 1952. Nuxhall enjoyed a 15-year big league career, then became a longtime Reds broadcaster.

THE OLDEST WAS SATCHEL PAIGE, AT 59.

The Negro leagues legend finally got his chance to pitch in the majors in 1948, when he was already 42. Despite his advanced age, he had a solid five-season run with the Indians and then the St. Louis Browns, making two All-Star teams. He retired after the 1953 season, but the Kansas City A's coaxed him out of retirement 12 years later as something of a publicity

stunt. Paige, then 59, sat on a rocking chair in the bullpen during a game against the Red Sox and was served coffee by an attendant dressed as a nurse. He ended up pitching three scoreless innings in the game. As he left the field, fans serenaded him with the song "The Old Gray Mare." He was inducted into the Hall of Fame in 1971.

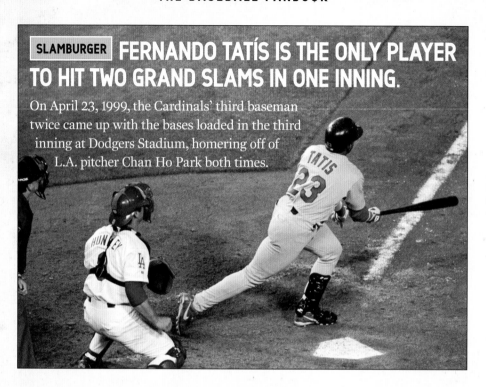

SLAMBURGER FERNANDO TATÍS IS THE ONLY PLAYER TO HIT TWO GRAND SLAMS IN ONE INNING.

On April 23, 1999, the Cardinals' third baseman twice came up with the bases loaded in the third inning at Dodgers Stadium, homering off of L.A. pitcher Chan Ho Park both times.

NO BACKS! THE DODGERS AND THE CUBS ONCE TRADED MINOR LEAGUE TEAMS.

The Brooklyn Dodgers were trying to pave the way for a potential move to Los Angeles. In order to stake their claim to L.A., they first had to take control of the city's Pacific Coast League team, which was owned by the Cubs. To make the swap work, the Dodgers gave the Cubs their Texas League team in Fort Worth, Texas, as well as the Pacific Coast League team they owned in Portland, Oregon. The big league clubs held on to a couple of prized prospects, but dozens of players moved between the L.A. and Portland teams because of the swap.

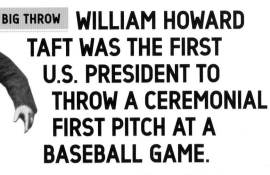

BIG THROW WILLIAM HOWARD TAFT WAS THE FIRST U.S. PRESIDENT TO THROW A CEREMONIAL FIRST PITCH AT A BASEBALL GAME.

The 27th president started the tradition in 1910 at the Washington Senators' season opener against the Philadelphia Athletics at American League Park. He threw to Senators star pitcher Walter Johnson, the starter that day. The ball was never put into play, but Taft later autographed it for Johnson at the pitcher's request.

WHAT ARE THE ODDS? A BATTER HIT A FAN WITH A FOUL BALL TWICE IN THE SAME AT BAT.

In August 1957, Alice Roth was watching her hometown Phillies play the New York Giants with her two grandsons. Philadelphia star Richie Ashburn hit a foul ball into the stands that struck Roth in the face, breaking her nose. Play stopped while she was attended to, then started again while she was being brought out of the stadium on a stretcher. Ashburn fouled off the next pitch, which struck Roth again, this time hitting her knee. Ashburn visited her at the hospital and the two became friends; Roth's grandsons were later invited to get a look at the Phillies' clubhouse.

CAUTION
Watch For
Batted Balls

HISTORY THE PITTSBURGH PIRATES WERE THE FIRST TEAM TO HAVE AN ALL BLACK AND LATINO LINEUP.

Jackie Robinson broke Major League Baseball's color barrier in 1947. On September 1, 1971, the Pittsburgh Pirates, led by future Hall of Famers Roberto Clemente and Willie Stargell, became the first team to field an all African-American and Latino starting lineup. Pittsburgh beat the Phillies 10–7 that day.

POPULAR VOTE DAVID ORTIZ FINISHED THIRD IN THE 2013 BOSTON MAYORAL RACE.

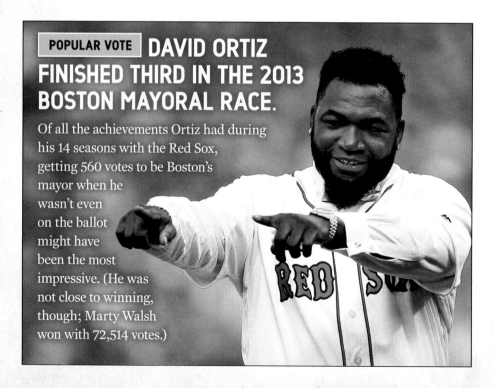

Of all the achievements Ortiz had during his 14 seasons with the Red Sox, getting 560 votes to be Boston's mayor when he wasn't even on the ballot might have been the most impressive. (He was not close to winning, though; Marty Walsh won with 72,514 votes.)

TIMEOUT

THE 1989 WORLD SERIES WAS DELAYED FOR 10 DAYS BECAUSE OF AN EARTHQUAKE.

That year's Series pitted the two teams from California's Bay Area—the A's and the Giants—against each other. About 30 minutes before Game 3 was scheduled to start, a deadly earthquake rocked the area, causing damage across both cities. The power was knocked out at San Francisco's Candlestick Park, which was hosting that night's game, and pieces of concrete fell from the upper deck. The game was immediately postponed and wasn't played until 10 days later. (The A's swept the Giants in four games.)

STUNTMAN

BILL VEECK HAD AN ODDBALL APPROACH.

The owner of three MLB franchises and one minor league club during his baseball life, Veeck was known for thinking outside the box. Some of his ideas were lasting. And others? Well....

Veeck's Top Five Gimmicks

1. The Littlest Leadoff Hitter. Veeck hired Eddie Gaedel *(near left),* a dwarf who stood 3'7", to pinch–hit in the bottom of the first for Veeck's St. Louis Browns in a 1951 game against the Detroit Tigers. Gaedel was rolled out in a papier–mâché cake, wearing uniform number ⅛.

2. A Clown of a Coach. Max Patkin, a performer known as the Clown Prince of Baseball, served as slapstick coach for Veeck's Browns, Indians, and White Sox.

3. Short Pants and Sox. In an August 1976 game, Veeck's White Sox took the field in shorts. They won, but the fashion trend never caught on; the shorts only made two more appearances.

4. When the Fans Managed. In 1951, Veeck decided to give Browns manager Zack Taylor a night off. While Taylor sat in a rocking chair, approximately 1,000 fans held up signs to instruct players what to do. And St. Louis won (5–3, over the Philadelphia Athletics).

5. Disco Demolition Night. Veeck and the White Sox wanted to bid farewell to the once–trendy music between games of a doubleheader against the Tigers in 1979. The plan was to blow up a box of disco records on the field. But the explosion damaged the field, and rowdy fans got carried away. The Sox had to forfeit the second game.

Veeck's Lasting Contributions

1. Integration of the American League. Jackie Robinson broke baseball's color line with the Dodgers of the NL in April 1947. Eleven weeks later, Veeck signed outfielder Larry Doby to the Indians as the first black player in the AL.

2. Stretch Time with Harry. One of the enduring images of fun at the ballpark is longtime announcer Harry Caray leading fans in signing "Take Me Out to the Ball Game" during the seventh-inning stretch. Caray is known for doing it at the Cubs' Wrigley Field, but Veeck had Caray begin the tradition when he was the White Sox' announcer.

3. Exploding Scoreboard. All those graphics you see pop up on the scoreboard at the ballpark? That was Veeck's idea, starting in 1960 at the White Sox' Comiskey Park.

4. Names on Jerseys. It was also Veeck's idea to start putting players' last names on the backs of jerseys, first done for the White Sox in 1960.

5. Ivy Idea. Before he was an owner, Veeck worked for the Cubs. In 1937 he was behind the planting of the iconic ivy that would cover the walls at Wrigley Field in an effort to give baseball a "day at the park" feel.

TRIFECTA JESÚS, MATTY, AND FELIPE ALOU ARE THE ONLY TRIO OF BROTHERS TO PLAY IN THE SAME OUTFIELD AT THE SAME TIME.

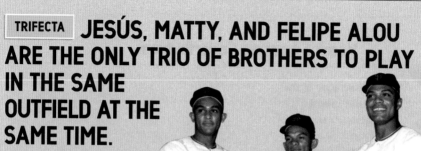

It happened when they were playing for the Giants in September 1963. Felipe *(far right)* started a game against the Mets, and later on his brothers, Jesús *(near right)* and Matty *(center)*, entered as defensive replacements.

DIRTY BUSINESS ROAD TEAMS BEGAN WEARING GRAY UNIFORMS BECAUSE THEY DIDN'T HAVE TIME TO DO LAUNDRY WHEN THEY WERE ON THE ROAD.

The home team has traditionally worn white in baseball, while the road team dresses in gray. It started in the game's early days, when teams on road trips didn't always have the ability to wash their uniforms and wore the darker color to hide dirt.

U.S.A+ **ALBERT PUJOLS HAD A PERFECT SCORE ON HIS U.S. CITIZENSHIP TEST.**

After leading the Cardinals to the 2006 World Series title, Pujols found some time to hit the books. He was born in the Dominican Republic but moved to Missouri when he was 16. With his wife, Deirdre, tutoring him, Pujols took the U.S. citizenship test in February 2007 and scored a perfect 100, officially becoming an American citizen.

SEPARATED AT BIRTH? MIKE TROUT AND BRYCE HARPER HIT THEIR 150TH HOME RUNS AT THE EXACT SAME AGE.

Trout and Harper have quite a bit in common as otherworldly talents who took the baseball world by storm at a very young age. They also share something else: Both were exactly 24 years and 295 days old when they hit their 150th career home runs.

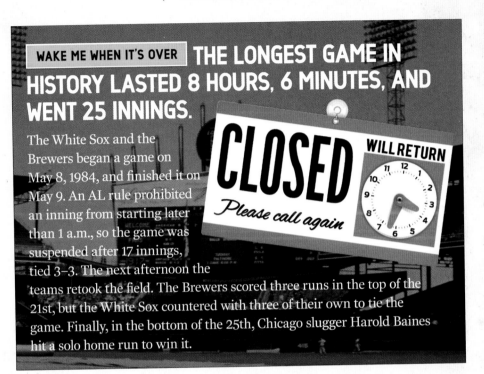

WAKE ME WHEN IT'S OVER # THE LONGEST GAME IN HISTORY LASTED 8 HOURS, 6 MINUTES, AND WENT 25 INNINGS.

The White Sox and the Brewers began a game on May 8, 1984, and finished it on May 9. An AL rule prohibited an inning from starting later than 1 a.m., so the game was suspended after 17 innings, tied 3–3. The next afternoon the teams retook the field. The Brewers scored three runs in the top of the 21st, but the White Sox countered with three of their own to tie the game. Finally, in the bottom of the 25th, Chicago slugger Harold Baines hit a solo home run to win it.

BLINK AND YOU'LL MISS IT # THE FASTEST GAME IN HISTORY WAS 51 MINUTES.

The New York Giants made quick work of the Phillies at the Polo Grounds on September 28, 1919. Jesse Barnes threw a complete game for New York, Lee Meadows threw all eight innings for Philadelphia, and fans were headed home after less than an hour following a 6–1 Giants win.

BANNER YEAR 2017 FEATURED THE MOST HOME RUNS HIT IN AN MLB SEASON, AS WELL AS THE MOST STRIKEOUTS.

There was a pretty easygoing vibe for defensive players across baseball in 2017, as hitters were either swinging and missing (40,104 strikeouts) or blasting the ball into the seats (6,105 home runs). Yankees slugger Aaron Judge *(left)* led the AL in home runs (52) and the majors in strikeouts (208), while Marlins outfielder Giancarlo Stanton led all big leaguers with 59 homers. On the pitching side, Red Sox lefty Chris Sale's league-leading 308 strikeouts were the most by a pitcher in 15 years. His teammate Rick Porcello, on the other hand, served up more homers than any pitcher in baseball (38).

OOPS HANK AARON'S 1957 TOPPS CARD WAS ACCIDENTALLY INVERTED.

Aaron was known for his majestic righthanded swing, which made this card so unusual. The cardmakers at Topps accidentally ran a reversed image (you can see part of one of the backward 4's on his uniform) of the baseball legend. It's one of the most famous and rare "error" cards ever made.

CARD TRICK THE ORIGINAL TOPPS BASEBALL CARDS WERE SPLIT INTO A SET OF "RED BACKS" AND "BLUE BACKS," 52 APIECE, SO THAT KIDS COULD USE THEM TO PLAY GAMES.

When they were first manufactured, baseball cards were not meant to be collected and kept in plastic cases. They were meant to be played with.

LIKE FATHER, LIKE SON KEN GRIFFEY JR. AND KEN GRIFFEY SR. HIT BACK-TO-BACK HOMERS.

When the 40-year-old Griffey Sr. joined his son on the Mariners, they became the first father-son teammates in baseball history. And on September 14, 1990, facing California Angels pitcher Kirk McCaskill, Senior hit a home run as the game's second batter. Junior, who was 20, stepped to the plate next and hit another!

★ 63 ★

WHATEVER WORKS

JIMMY PIERSALL CELEBRATED HIS 100TH CAREER HOMER BY BACKPEDALING AROUND THE BASES.

Piersall was a talented player who also had some dark moments while battling bipolar disorder during his career. But this milestone brought up one of the lighter moments in baseball history. After hitting his only home run as a member of the Mets, he celebrated the long ball as no one ever had before, running from first to home—but backward.

TRÈS SENSITIVE ## ALL–STAR CATCHER BENITO SANTIAGO CHANGED HIS UNIFORM NUMBER FROM "9" TO "09."

It might be the strangest uniform number in the history of sports. Catching for the Padres in 1991, Santiago decided he didn't like the way the back strap of his chest protector felt atop the number 9 on his back. If he wore a double-digit number, the strap would have run between the two digits, not over a stitched-on number. But he didn't want to give up the number 9. So his solution was to turn a single-digit number into a double-digit one. He wore "09" for the Padres, then for two seasons with the Marlins.

Apparently he got over his sensitivity. Later in his career, he wore a "9" again, with the Cubs, and he wore "6" with the Reds.

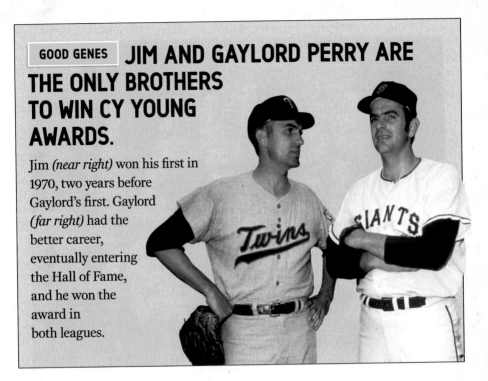

GOOD GENES **JIM AND GAYLORD PERRY ARE THE ONLY BROTHERS TO WIN CY YOUNG AWARDS.**

Jim *(near right)* won his first in 1970, two years before Gaylord's first. Gaylord *(far right)* had the better career, eventually entering the Hall of Fame, and he won the award in both leagues.

BAD TIMING **THE EXPOS WERE THE BEST TEAM THE YEAR THE WORLD SERIES WAS CANCELED.**

Montreal never won a world championship, but the Expos had a chance in 1994. They had baseball's best record on August 11 (74–40), when the players' strike went into effect. The rest of the season, including the playoffs and the World Series, was canceled. The next year injuries and cost-cutting trades led to a down year. The Expos finished last in the NL East in 1995 and never made the playoffs again. They relocated and became the Washington Nationals in 2005.

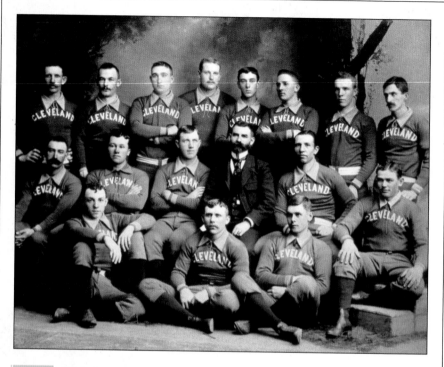

OY THE 1899 CLEVELAND SPIDERS WERE THE WORST TEAM IN MLB HISTORY.

The Spiders had actually enjoyed seven straight winning seasons heading into 1899, but club owners had just bought a second team, the St. Louis Perfectos. Owner Stanley Robinson planned to make the Spiders "a sideshow," and traded the Spiders' best players to St. Louis, including superstar pitcher Cy Young. The Spiders, left with scraps, drew fewer than 200 fans per game, and opposing teams started refusing to visit them since the money they'd make from their share of the ticket sales wouldn't cover travel costs. The Spiders were forced to play most of their games on the road (42 home games, 112 road games). They finished 20–134, with a .130 winning percentage, which is still the worst in baseball history, and folded after the season.

CY YOUNG

STRETCH

JON RAUCH WAS THE TALLEST PLAYER IN BIG LEAGUE HISTORY.

At 6' 11", he was an intimidating presence on the mound. And the list of teams Rauch pitched for during his 11-year career was about as long as his right arm: White Sox, Expos/Nationals, Diamondbacks, Twins, Blue Jays, Mets, and Miami Marlins. He found his niche as a relief pitcher, and even led the National League in games pitched in 2007 (88 for the Nationals).

SKILLS TO MASTER

Whether you're eager to snag an autograph or ready to perfect your slide into second, you need to know how to do things the right way—even eat sunflower seeds!

GET AN AUTOGRAPH

You can take your chances through the mail, but your best bet is to get a player's signature live and in-person at a game. Here are helpful hints.

1 BP isn't just for players Try to get to the stadium for batting practice; many parks open 90 minutes before the game. Some of them even have designated areas where players will sign. Try to get a spot right on the wall, as close to the dugout as possible. But don't push, and be respectful of the people who actually bought the tickets for those seats!

2 Put a name with the face "Hey, you!" and "Number 53!" won't often catch a player's attention. Know who's who and make your request personal. Be polite: Go with "Mr." instead of the player's first name, and always say "please" and (if you get the signature) "thank you."

3 Bring your own pen The players themselves won't carry one around. And, of course, don't get greedy—one signature per player. If a player doesn't sign, it's O.K. to be disappointed, but don't insult him. You might have better luck at another game or find it easier at the team's fan appreciation day or spring training.

BREAK IN A GLOVE

Usually, a new glove will be way too stiff to use right away. Here's how to get it game-ready.

1 Moisten the leather

Pour a small cup of warm water over any stiff part of the glove you want to loosen up.

2 Bend it

Get those fingers flexible so you can secure a catch. Flex the glove backward so that the inside pops out, or touch the top of the thumb and the pinkie to the middle of the mitt.

3 Hammer time

With the help of a parent, use a wooden mallet (or the end of a dumbbell weight) to pound a fold where you want to be able to bend the glove to make a catch. But don't wear it while you do it!

4 Rubber band aid

Put a ball in the pocket, and then put three or four rubber bands around it. Let it sit for a few hours (or overnight), then use the mallet again.

6 Love it!

Your glove is your best friend on the field, so treat it that way! Don't leave it on the dugout floor to get stepped on, and don't leave it outside when you get home.

5 Condition

It's optional, but you can try glove conditioner a couple of times over the course of the year to keep your mitt in good shape.

SCORE A GAME

There's no one right way to do it, but there are some universal symbols in the art of scorekeeping. For instance, the defensive positions, 1 through 9, are always the same. But it's up to you to decide what little flourishes and markings you might want to add to your score book. You'll get a souvenir from the game, plus keeping score is a great way to stay involved with every out. Or, almost every out. You can always use the marking that Yankees Hall of Fame shortstop turned broadcaster Phil Rizzuto used to use: "WW." It stands for "wasn't watching." To get a better idea of how to keep score, take a look at our sample inning, which features quite an impressive bunch of players.

KNOW THESE SYMBOLS

H = hit
E = error
K = strikeout swinging
Ж = strikeout looking
1B = single
2B = double
3B = triple
HR = home run
FC = fielder's choice
BB = walk (base on balls)
HP = hit by pitch
SB = stolen base
CS = caught stealing
WP = wild pitch
PB = passed ball
BK = balk
SF = sacrifice fly
SAC = sacrifice bunt
DP = double play
GIDP = grounded into double play
FO = foul out
U = unassisted putout

POSITION KEY

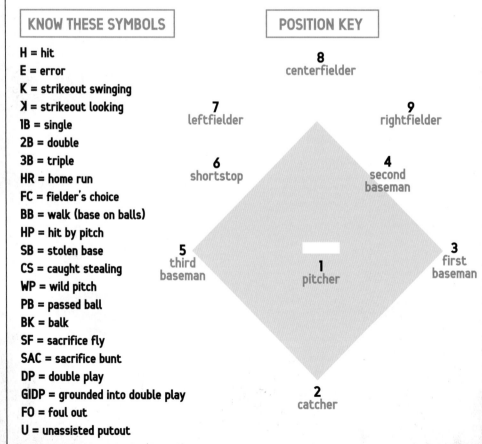

8
centerfielder

7
leftfielder

9
rightfielder

6
shortstop

4
second baseman

5
third baseman

1
pitcher

3
first baseman

2
catcher

Baseball Score Sheet

Superstar Team 1 _____ at ___ Superstar Team 2 ___ Date: 6/12/56

Weather: Hot and sunny _____ Time: 2 p.m.

#	PLAYER		WHAT HAPPENED
9	Ted Williams	E-5	Williams reached base on an error by the third baseman and then scored on Hank Aaron's home run.
44	Hank Aaron	HR	Aaron hit a home run.
42	Jackie Robinson	SB ⓓ H-7	Robinson hit a double to leftfield and stole third.
7	Mickey Mantle	6-3 ①	Mantle hit to the shortstop, who threw him out at first for the first out of the inning.
21	Roberto Clemente	② DP BB	Clemente walked and then was thrown out at second after Stan Musial hit into a double play.
6	Stan Musial	5-4-3 ③	Musial hit into a double play: third base to second to first.
	Totals	R 2 / H 2	

Circle outs as they are made: 1, 2, 3.
Move batters around the base paths by drawing the sides of a diamond.

CHEW SUNFLOWER SEEDS

It's a classic dugout snack, but you need practice to be able to separate the seed from the shell.

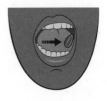

1 Put one seed in your mouth

It's not a meal. If you try to manage a mouthful of seeds, you will either end up swallowing a bunch of shells or spitting them all over yourself.

2 Move the seed to your left or right molars

Use your tongue to push it to one side or the other, positioning it at your back teeth.

3 Crack the seed

The edges (where the seed is split) should be touching your teeth. A little gentle pressure should open the seed.

4 Separate the inner seed from the shell

Using your tongue, separate the shell part (which you shouldn't eat) from the seed.

5 Spit out the shell

If it's O.K. with your coach and/or parents (if you're outside), just spit the seed on the ground. Otherwise spit it into a trash can.

6 Eat the seed

You've done it! You can now chew, swallow, and enjoy the prize. Just try not to make too much of a mess.

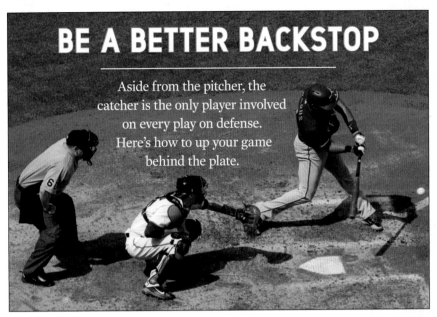

BE A BETTER BACKSTOP

Aside from the pitcher, the catcher is the only player involved on every play on defense. Here's how to up your game behind the plate.

▲ **Freeze frame** Framing a pitch is one of the most important things a catcher does—and it's something that many people never notice. Catch the pitch with your arm extended, elbow slightly bent, and as you catch it, subtly move your glove back toward the middle of the plate.

◄ **For the block** When you have to block a low pitch, don't panic. Without jumping out of your crouch, move down and forward toward the ball. As you block it, you should be on your knees with your glove covering the space between your legs.

► **Rise and fire** Footwork is the key to a good throw. Picture a triangle; when you crouch, each foot is one point, and the third point is a spot about a foot in front of you. As you catch the pitch, step your right foot (or left foot, if you're a lefty thrower) to the top of the triangle. That is your plant foot. Then step with your left and fire a throw.

GET A BALL AT A GAME

It's a free souvenir, and there are a bunch of them available. So bring your glove and—most important—keep your eye on the ball!

1 Location, location, location Face it: If you're sitting 450 feet away in dead centerfield, it's possible you could get a ball, but don't hold your breath. Fans are more likely to snag foul balls, which usually land somewhere in the first few sections about even with first or third base. A player will almost always foul the ball off toward the opposite field.

2 Warmup If you get to the game early, grab a spot near the wall just past the dugout around where players are warming up. (There are usually fewer fans on the visiting team's side.) If you ask nicely and call the player by name, he might flip you a ball when he's done with his pregame catch.

3 Three outs Usually after the third out of the inning, the player who caught that out (most often the first baseman) will flip the ball to a fan. If you can get a spot near the dugout, you have a chance at receiving a souvenir.

SLIDE

You've got the speed—now learn how to finish the right way
when taking that extra base.

1 Most slides start about four to six feet from the base, but practicing will show you how far you typically slide. You don't want to end up getting tagged out because you didn't make it to the base.

2 It doesn't matter which leg you "tuck" when you slide; do whatever is more comfortable to you. Stay low to the ground and keep your momentum going forward. Kick one foot toward the base. Fold the other leg underneath you and sit down.

3 Keep your tummy muscles tight and tense as you go down—that will prevent you from banging the back of your head on the ground. Your backside, not your thigh, should hit the dirt. Your lead foot should be slightly off the ground with toes pointing upward.

4 Your hands should remain in the air; putting a hand in the dirt will not only slow you down a bit, but it could also lead to a hand injury. Once you reach the base—safely—keep your foot on the base until you can ask an umpire for a timeout.

STAY FOCUSED

No one said it was easy being a fan. Baseball packs more games into a season than any professional sport. Here's how to stay engaged.

1 Phases of the game A game lasts nine innings, yes. But focus on the breakdowns within those nine innings. Is there a starting pitcher who typically fades late in his starts? Then the lineup's goal might be to score runs early, before the opposing team can go to its bullpen. Or is it a case where the starter is dominant but the bullpen is weak? Long at bats, even if they don't result in hits, could be turning points, as each pitch moves the starter closer to having to exit the game.

2 They all count Opening Day is fun, and late-season pennant races are great. But keep in mind: All those matchups count as much as the games in mid-June.

3 Minor interest Has your team fallen hopelessly out of contention? The future can still hold your interest. That means paying extra attention to the performance of young players, or even checking out a minor league game or two toward the end of the summer.

GET BETTER ON YOUR OWN

You don't need to take the field with eight teammates to work on your skills. Here's how you can do it solo, in your backyard or at your local park.

1 Hit off a tee If you're in a small space or sharing a crowded field, set up a net in front of you. Otherwise, you can get a bucket of balls and swing away. Repeating proper mechanics, even when the ball isn't moving, is key to becoming a consistently strong hitter.

2 Throw a tennis ball against the garage door Toss a bouncy ball (not a hard ball) against a wall or the side of your house, catch it with your glove, then make the transition to your throwing hand. Repeating this routine (faster and faster) will help you develop those fast hands for infield play.

3 Mark a spot on a wall, or on a practice net This can improve your pitching, or just your throwing accuracy. Use a net, or use a softer ball and pick out a spot on a wall or the side of your house. That's your target; hit it again and again.

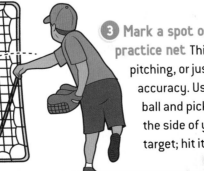

GET ON CAMERA

Just in case your friends don't believe you when you say you're going to the game, here's how to improve your chances of getting on TV.

1 Bring a sign As long as the stadium you're going to lets you bring one in, that is. (Check the rules online.) And, of course, if there are people sitting behind you, don't hold it up while the game is going on. Make your poster big and colorful—the more creative the better!

2 Seats to be seen Obviously, the fans sitting low and directly behind home plate will be on TV. But there are also plenty of camera shots of the hitter, with fans seated to the side of home plate (third base side for a righthanded hitter, first base side for a lefty) in view. The camera angles can be slightly different at each stadium, so pay attention to which seats actually show up on TV.

3 Always record It helps to have a friend or family member watching to confirm whether or not you made the broadcast, but either way, make sure you recorded the game so you can check when you get home.

SING "TAKE ME OUT TO THE BALL GAME"

After the third out of the top of the seventh inning, you'll get to show off those singing chops. Make sure you know the lyrics to this classic tune! (You'll hear the chorus of the song only, which starts midway through the fourth line below.)

Ka-tie Ca-sey was base-ball mad, Had the fe-ver and had it bad; Just to root for the home town crew, ev-'ry sou Ka-tie blew. On a Sa-tur-day, her young beau Called to see if she'd like to go, To see a show but Miss Kate said, "No! I'll tell you what you can do," Take me out to the ball game, Take me out with the crowd, Buy me some pea-nuts and Crac-ker Jack, I don't care if I ne-ver get back. Let me root, root, root for the home team, If they don't win it's a shame; For it's one, two, three strikes you're out, at the old ball game.

RECOGNIZE THESE GRIPS

(Note: Some of these advanced pitches can be dangerous for young, developing arms. Stick with fastballs and changeups.)

FOUR–SEAM FASTBALL

An old-fashioned heater, fairly straight and always fast.
BEST OF TODAY: Justin Verlander, Aroldis Chapman

TWO–SEAM FASTBALL

This fastball comes with a little less velocity but also downward motion, like a sinker.
BEST OF TODAY: Corey Kluber, Zach Britton

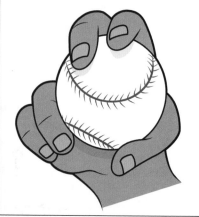

CURVEBALL

Pressure from the top fingers creates a tight spin, causing the ball to curve down toward the dirt.
BEST OF TODAY: Clayton Kershaw, Stephen Strasburg

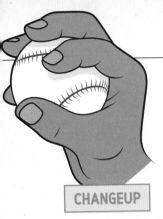

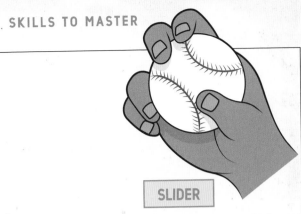

CHANGEUP

Holding the ball deeper in the grip (many use a "circle change," in which the thumb and index finger almost touch each other to essentially form a circle on the side of the ball) leads to arm action that says fastball—but a slower pitch that catches hitters off-guard.
BEST OF TODAY: Félix Hernández, Cole Hamels

SLIDER

A grip between a four-seam fastball and a curveball, this breaking pitch has more of a side-to-side break, with greater velocity than a curveball.
BEST OF TODAY: Max Scherzer, Andrew Miller

CUTTER

With a slightly off-center grip, this is a fastball with a late break, like a mini-slider.
BEST OF TODAY:
Kenley Jansen, Jon Lester

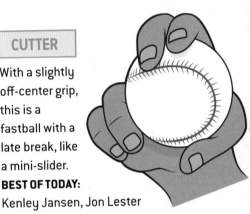

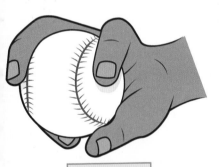

SPLITTER

The same concept as a forkball, which requires the middle and index fingers to be spread wide on the ball. The wrist is snapped downward on release, leading to a fastball that dives into the dirt at the last moment.
BEST OF TODAY:
Masahiro Tanaka

KNUCKLEBALL

A lack of any spin leads to this pitch moving unpredictably on its way to the plate.
BEST OF TODAY: R.A. Dickey

DRESS YOUR DOG

It's the must-have snack at any stadium. If you're watching the game from your house, here's how you (with the help of an adult) can re-create some of MLB's most famous dogs.

DODGER DOG
L.A. Dodgers
Since 1962 this 10-inch dog has been baseball's most famous. You'll typically find it covered in mustard, relish, and ketchup.

SUNRISE DOG
Kansas City Royals
A dog topped with bacon, a fried egg, cheese, and gravy. It's perfect for those earlier starts for weekend games (especially if you slept in).

THE HEATER
Chicago White Sox

Jalapeño cheddar sausage, spicy cole slaw, and sriracha mayo. (Remember, milk is better than water when it comes to dousing the heat of fiery foods!)

CRACKER JACK AND MAC DOG
Pittsburgh Pirates

Two baseball classics come together for one unforgettable (if maybe nonsensical) combination: a dog with mac and cheese *and* Cracker Jack.

CHICKEN ENCHILADAS DOG
Arizona Diamondbacks

A Southwestern twist: chicken enchilada sausage topped with queso blanco, enchilada sauce, pico de gallo, black olives, sour cream, and tortilla strips.

THE BROOMSTICK HOT DOG
Texas Rangers

You'd probably be making a miniaturized version of this two-foot monster dog—or inviting a few of your friends over to help you eat the real thing. It's topped with chili, nacho cheese, grilled onions, and jalapeños.

RUN A TEAM

Assemble a roster, then
survive the longest season
in professional sports.
This is how MLB
franchises are built.

The FRANCHISE

A baseball team has a bunch of hitters and a bunch of pitchers, the guys you see on TV or at the stadium 162 times over the course of a season. But a baseball franchise is made up of so many more people, most of whom don't hit,

TOM RICKETTS AND THEO EPSTEIN

pitch, throw, or run. Some of them work on the baseball side: managers for all the teams in the organization's farm system *(next page)* and numerous coaches and instructors at all levels. There are also the people who aren't in uniform, front-office employees (such as Cubs team president Theo Epstein) whose job it is to acquire those players and coaches, and decide how much they'll be paid. Then there are hundreds of other employees who handle the everyday jobs you might not think about: from scouts who put together reports on upcoming opponents or players to draft, to trainers who make sure players stay in top condition, to workers who make sure the home stadium is kept up throughout the long season. And every team has an owner (such as Tom Ricketts, whose family owns the Cubs) who oversees it all. This is just a glimpse into some of the different departments that make a Major League Baseball team work.

OFF THE FIELD

A baseball franchise is made up of hundreds
of people who don't take the field.

 BASEBALL OPERATIONS Often led by a general manager, this is the department in charge of deciding which players to acquire. The staff also has advance scouts who put together reports on upcoming opponents.

 PLAYER DEVELOPMENT This is typically the minor league staff, which is in charge of making sure minor league players are getting better.

 AMATEUR SCOUTING This department is in charge of checking out potential draft picks and international signees.

 MEDICAL/TRAINING STAFF These folks manage all aspects of the players' health, helping them recover from injuries and also stay strong throughout the season.

 BALLPARK OPERATIONS Staffers, including the grounds crew and security team, who make sure the home stadium is up to snuff.

THE FARM SYSTEM

Every franchise has a collection of minor league teams that consist mostly of young players; the primary focus is on developing them for the big leagues (though clubs try to win their games as well). Here are the teams that made up the Chicago Cubs' farm system in 2017, from the highest to the lowest level.

IOWA CUBS

TRIPLE A: Iowa Cubs (Pacific Coast League)
DOUBLE A: Tennessee Smokies (Southern League)
CLASS A ADVANCED: Myrtle Beach Pelicans (Carolina League)
CLASS A: South Bend Cubs (Midwest League)
CLASS A SHORT SEASON: Eugene Emeralds (Northwest League)
ROOKIE LEAGUE: Arizona League Cubs (Arizona League)
FOREIGN ROOKIE LEAGUE: Dominican Summer League Cubs (Dominican Summer League)

Build a ROSTER

During school recess, two captains pick eight players apiece and you have your baseball teams. Roster building in Major League Baseball is a little more complicated. Below are the most common ways that teams acquire players, including examples of each for the 2017 World Series champion Houston Astros.

The MLB Draft

The team with the worst record the previous season picks first; the team with the best regular-season record picks last. There are a couple of twists: Only players from the United States, U.S. territories, and Canada can be drafted. That includes players from high school and junior/community college and also four-year college athletes who have played three seasons or turned 21. The draft has 40 rounds, and rarely do players *not* start their pro career in the minor leagues.

ASTROS EXAMPLE: Carlos Correa was the first overall pick of the 2012 first-year player draft. He graduated from Puerto Rico Baseball Academy and High School and made his big league debut in June 2015.

Trades

We see this all the time. One team is prepping for a pennant race, looking to make a big addition late in the year. Another team is out of contention, with some big-time players earning big-time money on the roster. So the two teams make a swap: an expensive star going to the contender, and a promising young prospect heading to the rebuilding team. Trades don't have to be player for player. Teams can swap certain kinds of draft picks or even a "player to be named later," which the teams agree on after one half of the deal has been completed.

ASTROS EXAMPLE: On August 31, 2017, Houston acquired Justin Verlander from the Detroit Tigers in exchange for three minor league prospects.

Free Agents

Teams often do all they can to retain their best players before they become free agents, meaning they have fulfilled their contracts and can sign with any team. But sometimes, especially for small-market teams, a player just wants more money than the team can afford. That's when the player hits the open market, spurring a bidding war among any interested teams.

ASTROS EXAMPLE: In November 2016, Houston signed free-agent outfielder Josh Reddick to a four-year, $52 million deal.

International Free Agents

In baseball, overseas players are not part of the draft like they are in the NBA. Teams have a set amount of money called a bonus pool that they can spend on international free agents under the age of 25. (Older players are exempt from the pool.) There are also specific rules with some professional leagues in Japan and South Korea, a "posting" system in which MLB clubs pay foreign teams for the right to negotiate with players. Athletes as young as 16 can be signed.

ASTROS EXAMPLE: José Altuve was signed when he was 17 years old for a $15,000 signing bonus after a tryout at the Astros' facility in his native Venezuela.

The Road to Free Agency

You might hear the term *under team control* regarding a player who is early in his career. What does it mean? Typically a player is not eligible for free agency until he has played six seasons in the majors. The first three years of a big league career are played for a relatively small salary set by the team. After that, a player is eligible for "arbitration." That means his salary is based on his performance. (A negotiation between the player and the team may take place.) However, some young players, known as Super 2, play enough in their first two seasons that they qualify for arbitration (and more money) in their third year. That's why some teams hold back top prospects and call them up in, say, May or June, to avoid the players becoming eligible for Super 2 status.

In-game STRATEGY

So you want to be a manager? It's harder than it looks. Over an incredibly long season (162 games!), managers have to figure out how to win as many matchups as possible by maximizing their players' performances. Here's a big-picture view of what a big league manager does for a team.

What kind of team are you?

This is often the decision of the front office as much as it is the manager. Large-market teams tend to have more money at their disposal, so they can just acquire the best players available. But teams in smaller markets have to spend their money wisely. They usually establish a specific team philosophy based on what kind of players are in their farm systems, the caliber and style of players they can acquire, and what type of ballpark they play in. Take the Orioles, for example. A mid-market team, they have collected a lot of power hitters to take advantage of homer-friendly Oriole Park at Camden Yards. Manager Buck Showalter rarely has his players steal bases, relying on the long ball to score runs. Conversely, the Royals play in a spacious home park and are loaded with speedier, more athletic players. They're aggressive on the base paths. And they try to sign pitchers who get batters to hit the ball in the air, because a lot of hits that would be over the fence in smaller parks turn into long outs in Kansas City's Kauffman Stadium.

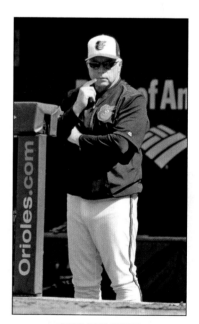

BUCK SHOWALTER

Setting the Lineup

It seems like an important job, but analysis has shown that the way a manager sets a lineup has little effect on the outcome of the game. For years managers preferred to bat a speedster in the leadoff spot, with someone who could make contact or bunt hitting second, followed by power hitters. These days, speed is still preferred at the top of the lineup. But most teams use leadoff hitters who get on base frequently and show patience at the plate, helping wear a pitcher down. And many teams now put their best hitters second in order to get them more plate appearances.

Defensive Positioning

It has become a major emphasis for teams in recent years. With "spray chart" data (which shows where each individual batter most often hits the ball) available across baseball, teams will often use dramatic shifts. In the photo, notice there are three infielders on the left side of the infield and only a first baseman on the right.

Bullpen Use

Especially because of the length of the season, bullpen use is crucial to being a successful manager. Part of using the bullpen well is knowing when to make a change. Over the course of the game, starting pitchers tend to become less effective as they tire and as opposing hitters get used to them. Managers also must determine which relief pitcher is right for which situation. Righthanded pitchers have more success against righthanded batters, and lefthanded pitchers have more success against lefties. But the manager must be careful not to burn through his bullpen too early, leaving him without his best relievers in the late innings. He also needs to keep in mind that relief pitchers wear down if they are used in several consecutive games.

Understanding ADVANCED STATISTICS

A round the turn of the 21st century, advanced stats started to become mainstream with baseball fans. The fact is, there was a time when batting average and ERA were considered advanced stats. Not anymore. Here are some of the new and best ways of evaluating player performance.

OPS+

ADJUSTED ON-BASE PERCENTAGE PLUS SLUGGING PERCENTAGE

MIKE TROUT

One of the simplest ways to gauge a hitter's effectiveness is to add together two basic stats. On-base percentage measures how frequently a batter reaches safely. Slugging percentage tells how many total bases a hitter averages per at bat. The sum of the two numbers is called OPS. It is a valuable tool for evaluating a hitter because it takes into account all aspects of hitting. OPS+ goes one step further. It compares a player's OPS to other players', with an OPS+ of 100 equaling the league average. This makes it easier to compare players across eras to see who was more dominant in their day. In 2017, Mike Trout led the majors in OPS+ for the second straight year, with a 187 mark. (The lowest OPS+ in 2017 belonged to Royals outfielder Alex Gordon, at 63.)

FIP

FIELDING INDEPENDENT PITCHING

COREY KLUBER

For many years, ERA (earned runs allowed per nine innings pitched) was the most important stat for pitchers. Now, FIP is considered a more accurate measure of effectiveness. While some elite pitchers have shown an ability to consistently force weak contact from hitters, most have little control over whether or not the fielders behind them turn a batted ball into an out. Stats show that, for a typical pitcher, about 30% of balls put into play will fall for a hit. (That doesn't count home runs, which his fielders have no chance of catching.) But that 30% number will be affected by luck. Some hard-hit balls will get caught, while weak hits sometimes sneak past defenders. FIP calculates what a pitcher's ERA would be if he allowed a league batting average (around .300) on balls in play. For instance, in 2017, Corey Kluber of the Indians was first in the AL in ERA (2.25), but his FIP was higher (2.50). Why? Only 26.8% of balls in play fell for hits, suggesting some luck for the Indians' ace.

UZR

ULTIMATE ZONE RATING

The easiest way to judge a fielder has always been to look at how many errors he makes. However, one defender might make an error on a play that a slower person wouldn't get to at all; the slower fielder's inability to make the play won't show up on the stat sheet. UZR gives the quicker defender credit for getting to a ball that another guy couldn't. Calculated by Fangraphs.com, it's a measure of approximately how many runs a player's defense saves over the course of a season. In 2017, Angels shortstop Andrelton Simmons led all infielders with a 15.5 UZR, meaning he saved about 15 runs that would have scored if the Angels had used a league-average defensive shortstop.

ANDRELTON SIMMONS

Be the MANAGER

Strategies have changed over the years, but managers still have plenty of important decisions to make every time their teams take the field.

Why do teams not bunt as much as they used to?

There was a time when teams tried to generate offense by moving runners around the diamond one base at a time, using bunts and stolen bases. Now that's known as small ball. It still has a place in Major League Baseball, but today's offenses rely heavily on the home run, while trying to conserve outs. Statistical analysis shows that attempting to sacrifice bunt, in which the offense trades an out to move a base runner (or runners) up one base, is a less efficient approach to scoring runs than just letting a batter swing away. There are exceptions, of course—if a batter is overmatched, like a pitcher coming to the plate in a National League game, the sac bunt is still the way to go. Ditto for some late-game situations when only one run is needed. But 2017 was the first time in the World Series era (dating back to 1903) that there were fewer than 1,000 sacrifice bunts during a season. And since players are asked to bunt less, many of them are not able to do it well. The 2017 season was also the year that featured the most home runs (6,105) and strikeouts (40,104). As frustrating as a strikeout can be, there are worse alternatives: A batter can hit into a double play. Or he can make an out on the first pitch, which makes the opposing pitcher's life easier. (On a strikeout, a pitcher has to throw at least three pitches.) And despite the record number of strikeouts, 2017 was still one of the higher-scoring seasons in MLB history, in part because the aggressive, all-or-nothing swings produce more home runs.

JOSH REDDICK

PAT NESHEK

Why do managers sometimes sit lefthanded hitters when they're going up against a lefthanded pitcher?

It's all about "picking up" the ball. Because of where a pitcher releases the ball, a batter who swings from the same side (a lefty facing a lefty, or a righty facing a righty) doesn't see the ball until a fraction of a second later than he would against a pitcher throwing from the opposite side. And the ball will move away from a lefty batter facing a lefty (same for a righty facing a righty), more so on a breaking ball. Because of that, managers will often use a pinch hitter (or change pitchers) to get a favorable lefty or righty matchup late in the game.

Pitchers who throw with lower arm angles can be even tougher for same-side hitters to face. For instance, reliever Pat Neshek, a two-time All-Star, is especially tough on righties because of his sidearm delivery. (Righties have a .187 batting average against him over his 11-year career.)

Starting pitchers used to throw complete games all the time. Why is that now a rarity?

Bullpens today are stronger than ever, partly because everyone throws harder, and also players are groomed to be relievers as early as college. (It used to be that relievers were guys who couldn't hack it as starters.) And a hitter will have an easier time against a pitcher the more times he faces him over the course of a game. But the biggest reason complete games have become so rare (there were only 59 in 2017, down from 266 two decades earlier) is the way pitchers are conditioned in the modern game. In the minor leagues, most are kept on a strict pitch count to protect their arms. So once a player reaches the majors, throwing an exorbitant number of pitches can lead to injury since the arm isn't used to it. The average starter tops out around 100 pitches, but in 2012, Mets ace Johan Santana threw a career-high 134 pitches during the first no-hitter in franchise history. He had never thrown more than 125 in an outing before then. Afterward, a shoulder injury he had struggled with resurfaced, and he made only 10 more starts in 2012. Santana was 33 years old, but that ended up being his final MLB season.

JOHAN SANTANA

Chapter 5

HE REMINDS ME OF...

Your grandparents have
déjà vu all over again when they
see these modern players on
the diamond. Which stars
of today play like the
stars of yesteryear?

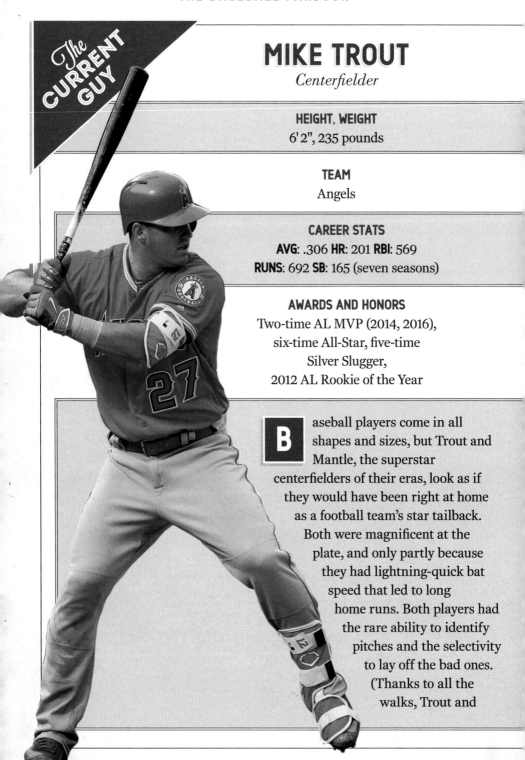

The **CURRENT GUY**

MIKE TROUT
Centerfielder

HEIGHT, WEIGHT
6' 2", 235 pounds

TEAM
Angels

CAREER STATS
AVG: .306 **HR**: 201 **RBI**: 569
RUNS: 692 **SB**: 165 (seven seasons)

AWARDS AND HONORS
Two-time AL MVP (2014, 2016),
six-time All-Star, five-time
Silver Slugger,
2012 AL Rookie of the Year

B aseball players come in all shapes and sizes, but Trout and Mantle, the superstar centerfielders of their eras, look as if they would have been right at home as a football team's star tailback. Both were magnificent at the plate, and only partly because they had lightning-quick bat speed that led to long home runs. Both players had the rare ability to identify pitches and the selectivity to lay off the bad ones. (Thanks to all the walks, Trout and

MICKEY MANTLE
Centerfielder

The OLD GUY

HEIGHT, WEIGHT
5'11", 195 pounds

TEAM
Yankees

CAREER STATS
AVG: .298 **HR**: 536 **RBI**: 1,509
RUNS: 1,676 **SB**: 153 (18 seasons)

AWARDS AND HONORS
Three-time AL MVP (1956, 1957,
1962), 20-time All-Star,
seven-time World Series champion,
1956 Triple Crown winner

Mantle have career on-base percentages over
.400.) And they were speedy runners. While
Mantle's stolen-base numbers weren't
eye-popping, he was known for getting
from the batter's box to first base faster
than anyone in baseball (estimated by
some at an amazing three seconds).
In today's game, Trout gets to
first as fast as anyone. That
speed translates to
exceptional defense as well:
Trout and Mantle could
each stake a claim to
being the best
all-around player
of his era.

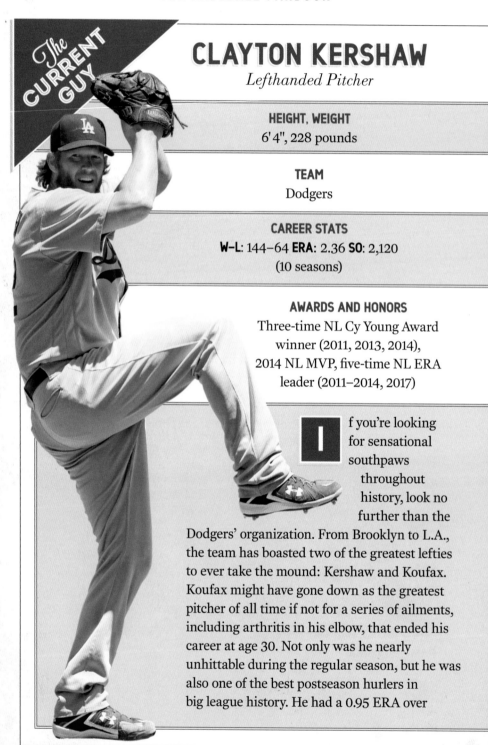

CLAYTON KERSHAW
Lefthanded Pitcher

HEIGHT, WEIGHT
6' 4", 228 pounds

TEAM
Dodgers

CAREER STATS
W–L: 144–64 **ERA:** 2.36 **SO:** 2,120
(10 seasons)

AWARDS AND HONORS
Three-time NL Cy Young Award
winner (2011, 2013, 2014),
2014 NL MVP, five-time NL ERA
leader (2011–2014, 2017)

If you're looking for sensational southpaws throughout history, look no further than the Dodgers' organization. From Brooklyn to L.A., the team has boasted two of the greatest lefties to ever take the mound: Kershaw and Koufax. Koufax might have gone down as the greatest pitcher of all time if not for a series of ailments, including arthritis in his elbow, that ended his career at age 30. Not only was he nearly unhittable during the regular season, but he was also one of the best postseason hurlers in big league history. He had a 0.95 ERA over

SANDY KOUFAX
Lefthanded Pitcher

The OLD GUY

HEIGHT, WEIGHT
6' 2", 210 pounds

TEAM
Dodgers

CAREER STATS
W–L: 165–87 **ERA**: 2.76 **SO**: 2,396
(12 seasons)

AWARDS AND HONORS
Three-time NL Cy Young Award winner
(1963, 1965, 1966), 1963 NL MVP,
two-time World Series MVP
(1963, 1965)

57 innings pitched in World Series games. Kershaw hasn't had that level of postseason dominance yet, but there are plenty of similarities in style between the two aces. They used over-the-top deliveries and high leg kicks that made it even trickier for opposing batters to see the ball coming out of their hands. Their repertoires each included fastballs that could reach well over 90 miles per hour. But the best pitch for both was an otherworldly curveball, two of the best ever thrown. They made their MLB debuts at an especially young age—Koufax was 19 when he joined the Dodgers, and Kershaw was 20. And they each had three NL Cy Young Awards before they turned 30.

JOSÉ ALTUVE

Second Baseman

HEIGHT, WEIGHT
5' 6", 165 pounds

TEAM
Astros

CAREER STATS
AVG: .316 HR: 84 RBI: 403
RUNS: 561
SB: 231 (seven seasons)

AWARDS AND HONORS
2017 AL MVP,
five-time All-Star,
three-time AL batting champion
(2014, 2016, 2017)

G oing all the way back to Babe Ruth, baseball's larger-than-life offensive stars have often been, well, large. But these two serve as a reminder that good things do, indeed, come in small packages. Both have been considered on-base machines, though in different ways. Altuve hammers base hits all over the ballpark, while Morgan drew plenty of walks. Morgan also packed a surprising amount of power into his small frame. He was a solid young player in Houston before being traded to Cincinnati, where he became a superstar as part of the Big Red Machine dynasty. He topped 20 home runs in a season four times in his

JOE MORGAN
Second Baseman

The OLD GUY

HEIGHT, WEIGHT
5'7", 160 pounds

TEAMS
Colt .45s/Astros, Reds, Giants, Phillies, A's

CAREER STATS
AVG: .271 **HR**: 268 **RBI**: 1,133
RUNS: 1,650 **SB**: 689
(22 seasons)

AWARDS AND HONORS
Two-time
NL MVP
(1975, 1976),
10-time All-Star

career and had 13 seasons with double-digit long balls. Like Morgan, Altuve has surprising pop considering he's one of the smallest players in baseball today. He had back-to-back 20-home-run seasons in 2016 and 2017. One other area in which these two are very similar? Their exciting style of play. Both were athletic, slick-fielding second basemen; both were terrors on the base paths. Morgan had nine consecutive 40-steal seasons from 1969 through 1977. Altuve stole at least 30 bases in each of his first six full MLB seasons and led the American League in steals in 2014 and 2015.

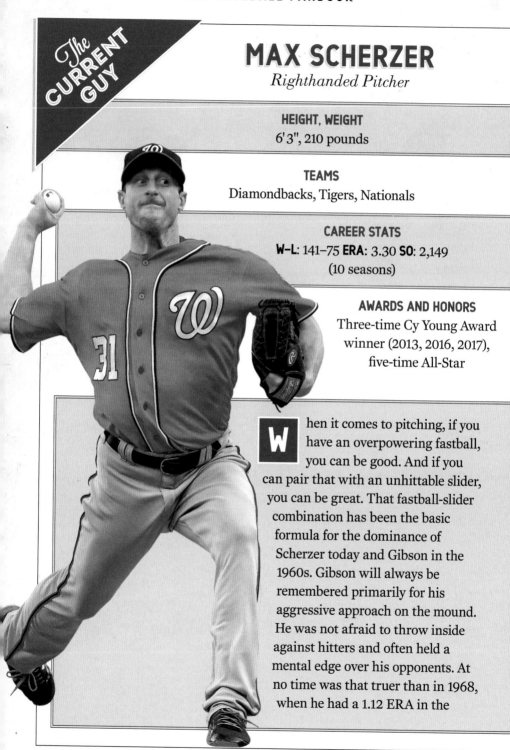

The CURRENT GUY

MAX SCHERZER
Righthanded Pitcher

HEIGHT, WEIGHT
6'3", 210 pounds

TEAMS
Diamondbacks, Tigers, Nationals

CAREER STATS
W–L: 141–75 **ERA:** 3.30 **SO:** 2,149
(10 seasons)

AWARDS AND HONORS
Three-time Cy Young Award
winner (2013, 2016, 2017),
five-time All-Star

When it comes to pitching, if you have an overpowering fastball, you can be good. And if you can pair that with an unhittable slider, you can be great. That fastball-slider combination has been the basic formula for the dominance of Scherzer today and Gibson in the 1960s. Gibson will always be remembered primarily for his aggressive approach on the mound. He was not afraid to throw inside against hitters and often held a mental edge over his opponents. At no time was that truer than in 1968, when he had a 1.12 ERA in the

BOB GIBSON
Righthanded Pitcher

THE OLD GUY

HEIGHT, WEIGHT
6'1", 189 pounds

TEAM
Cardinals

CAREER STATS
W–L: 251–174 **ERA**: 2.91
SO: 3,117 (17 seasons)

AWARDS AND HONORS
Two-time NL Cy Young Award winner
(1968, 1970), 1968 NL MVP, two-time
World Series MVP (1964, 1967),
nine-time All-Star

greatest single-season performance by a
pitcher since 1914. When Scherzer was
drafted 11th by the Diamondbacks in
2006, he was considered a potential closer
due to his fantastic fastball-slider
combination. His lack of a third pitch, and
his relatively low delivery, made it unclear
whether he could ever become a
big league starter. But he added a
changeup to his arsenal, and by the
time he was in his late 20s, he was
completely dominant for the Tigers.
Now with the Nationals, the durable
Scherzer is a true ace, capable of
shutting down an opponent on any
given night.

CHRIS SALE
Lefthanded Pitcher

HEIGHT, WEIGHT
6'6", 180 pounds

TEAMS
White Sox, Red Sox

CAREER STATS
W–L: 91–58 **ERA:** 2.98 **SO:** 1,552
(eight seasons)

AWARDS AND HONORS
Six-time All-Star,
two-time AL strikeout leader
(2015, 2017)

There are few things more intimidating for a batter than standing in against a pitcher who's not only hard-throwing, but tall as well. With Sale and Johnson, their height and long arms have made it look as if they were reaching out halfway to the plate before they unleashed a pitch. Johnson, nicknamed the Big Unit, was one of the most unusual and intimidating pitchers in baseball history. He was the size of a basketball center and threw a fastball that often touched 100 miles per hour on the radar gun. His career got off to a slow start due to control problems (he walked 100-plus

RANDY JOHNSON
Lefthanded Pitcher

The OLD GUY

HEIGHT, WEIGHT
6'10", 225 pounds

TEAMS
Expos, Mariners, Diamondbacks,
Yankees, Giants

CAREER STATS
W–L: 303–166 **ERA:** 3.29 **SO:** 4,875
(22 seasons)

AWARDS AND HONORS
Five-time Cy Young Award winner (1995,
1999–2002), 2001 World Series co-MVP,
nine-time league strikeout leader

batters in
each of his
first three
full seasons with the Mariners,
1990–1992), but by the time he had honed
his incredible stuff, he was unhittable.
Sale doesn't throw quite as hard as Johnson
did in his prime, though Sale's heater is
outstanding. But both pitchers have racked
up a ton of K's with devastating sliders.
Along with being very tall, both Johnson
and Sale pitched with low arm slots,
meaning they threw closer to sidearm than
over-the-top. That meant their sliders
darted to the left, with a big, late break that
rendered hitters helpless.

The **CURRENT GUY**

ANDRELTON SIMMONS
Shortstop

HEIGHT, WEIGHT
6' 2", 200 pounds

TEAMS
Braves, Angels

CAREER STATS
AVG: .264 **HR**: 49
RBI: 281 **RUNS**: 322
SB: 45 (six seasons)

AWARDS AND HONORS
Three-time Gold Glove Award winner
(2013, 2014, 2017)

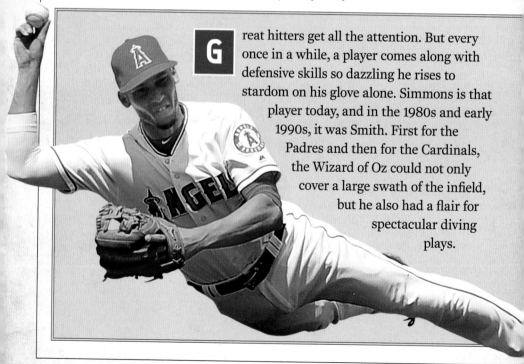

Great hitters get all the attention. But every once in a while, a player comes along with defensive skills so dazzling he rises to stardom on his glove alone. Simmons is that player today, and in the 1980s and early 1990s, it was Smith. First for the Padres and then for the Cardinals, the Wizard of Oz could not only cover a large swath of the infield, but he also had a flair for spectacular diving plays.

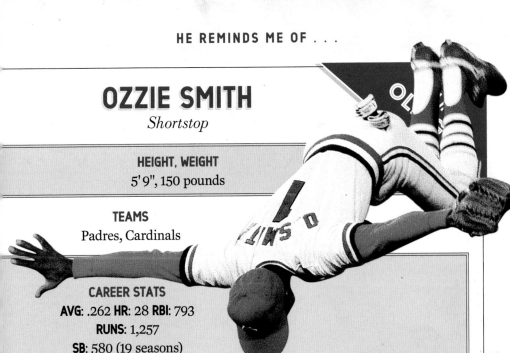

OZZIE SMITH
Shortstop

HEIGHT, WEIGHT
5'9", 150 pounds

TEAMS
Padres, Cardinals

CAREER STATS
AVG: .262 **HR**: 28 **RBI**: 793
RUNS: 1,257
SB: 580 (19 seasons)

AWARDS AND HONORS
13-time Gold Glove Award winner (1980–1992),
15-time All-Star

As a rookie in 1978, he once dived to snare a sharp ground ball, only to have it take a bad hop and deflect back behind him. Mid-dive, he managed to reach back with his bare hand, snag the ball, and throw the runner out at first. His trademark backflips when he took the field and sunny, infectious personality made him one of baseball's undisputed superstars, despite the fact that he hit just 28 home runs over his entire career. No one could match Smith's defensive prowess until Simmons. He's a bit of a different style of player, and he's much bigger. But he's also an athlete *and* an acrobat, which allows him to cover a ton of ground at shortstop. Like Smith, he turns in highlight-reel plays again and again. And like Smith, he's a better hitter than he sometimes gets credit for. Smith had six seasons with an on-base percentage better than .350. Simmons had an OPS (on-base percentage plus slugging percentage) of .752 in 2017, making him a solid offensive shortstop in addition to being the best at his position in the field.

BUSTER POSEY
Catcher

HEIGHT, WEIGHT
6'1", 215 pounds

TEAM
Giants

CAREER STATS
AVG: .308 **HR**: 128 **RBI**: 594
RUNS: 505 (nine seasons)

AWARDS AND HONORS
2012 NL MVP, five-time All-Star,
three-time World Series champion

Squatting behind home plate isn't the most glamorous job in baseball. But from calling and framing pitches, to throwing out base runners, to performing at the plate, catchers are more involved in a game than any player on the field. It's no surprise that great teams often have great catchers. Posey is the heart and soul of a Giants team that has won three World Series. Berra, who played for the Yankees' dynasty of the 1950s, will always be best remembered for his wacky

YOGI BERRA

Catcher

OLD GUY *The*

HEIGHT, WEIGHT
5'7", 185 pounds

TEAMS
Yankees, Mets

CAREER STATS
AVG: .285 **HR**: 358 **RBI**: 1,430
RUNS: 1,175 (19 seasons)

AWARDS AND HONORS
Three-time AL MVP (1951, 1954, 1955),
18-time All-Star,
10-time World Series champion

Yogi-isms, his trademark, off-the-wall observations. (Example: Baseball is 90% mental. The other half is physical.) But he was also an expert game-caller who made all the pitchers on the Yankees' staff better. Berra was MVP-caliber at the plate as well, capable of hitting for average and power. Posey is built differently than the short, compact Berra, and Posey plays in a much more competitive era. But he brings the same kind of leadership that made Berra an all-time great—even if Posey's interviews aren't quite as funny.

The CURRENT GUY

JUSTIN VERLANDER
Righthanded Pitcher

HEIGHT, WEIGHT
6'5", 225 pounds

TEAMS
Tigers, Astros

CAREER STATS
W–L: 188–114 **ERA:** 3.46 **SO:** 2,416
(13 seasons)

AWARDS AND HONORS
2011 AL Cy Young Award winner,
2011 AL MVP, four-time
AL strikeout leader
(2009, 2011, 2012, 2016)

For all the different pitches that have come into existence over the history of baseball, none can match the pure power of a great fastball. And for Verlander and Ryan, once they learned to harness the power of their heat, they became unstoppable. Verlander evolved into a superstar when he started locating his fastball better. In his first seasons he often just tried to throw his heater over the plate, blowing it by hitters. It worked sometimes, but not all the time. Then he started painting the corners with 100-mph heat and pairing his fastball with a devastating power curveball. That's when

NOLAN RYAN
Righthanded Pitcher

OLD GUY *The*

HEIGHT, WEIGHT
6' 2", 170 pounds

TEAMS
Mets, Angels, Astros, Rangers

CAREER STATS
W–L: 324–292 **ERA**: 3.19
SO: 5,714 (27 seasons)

AWARDS AND HONORS
11-time league strikeout
leader, MLB all-time leader
in strikeouts and no-hitters

he became as dominant as Ryan, another one of those rare pitchers who could break the 100-mph mark. Ryan came into the big leagues throwing hard, regularly topping 100 miles per hour, but not always throwing strikes. (He's the only pitcher post-1900 to have two 200-walk seasons.) But Ryan's command improved, and along with a power curveball and rare durability, he was often virtually unhittable. In fact, his seven career no-hitters still stands as an MLB record.

The
CURRENT
GUY

KENLEY JANSEN

Righthanded Pitcher

HEIGHT, WEIGHT
6'5", 275 pounds

TEAM
Dodgers

CAREER STATS
SAVES: 230 **ERA:** 2.08
(eight seasons)

AWARDS AND HONORS
Two-time All-Star
(2016, 2017)

T he toughest pitch in today's game belongs to the most dominant closer, Jansen. The burly righthander is nearly unhittable, holding opponents to an on-base percentage of just .234 over his first eight seasons. His trademark pitch: the cut fastball. To the hitter, it looks like a normal 98-mile-per-hour heater (as normal as a 98-mph heater *could* look) until it darts to the left at the last moment. It's the same pitch that made Rivera the

MARIANO RIVERA
Righthanded Pitcher

The OLD GUY

HEIGHT, WEIGHT
6' 2", 195 pounds

TEAM
Yankees

CAREER STATS
SAVES: 652
ERA: 2.21 (19 seasons)

AWARDS AND HONORS
13-time All-Star, 1999 World Series
MVP, five-time World Series
champion, MLB career saves leader

greatest closer in history. Rivera has a
different body type, but he was just as
dominant. When he was in his final
season, the Twins presented the
legendary closer with a gift in honor of
his upcoming retirement: a rocking
chair made out of broken bats. The joke
was that Rivera's cutter had destroyed
many bats; for lefthanded batters who
didn't swing and miss, the ball often
made contact with a low, weaker part
of the wood, causing it to shatter.
Jansen throws his cutter a little
harder than Rivera did, and the
outcome is usually the same: a lot
of frustrated hitters and a lot
of saves.

The CURRENT GUY

BRYCE HARPER
Rightfielder

HEIGHT, WEIGHT
6'3", 215 pounds

TEAM
Nationals

CAREER STATS
AVG: .285 **HR**: 150 **RBI**: 421
RUNS: 507 **SB**: 62 (six seasons)

AWARDS AND HONORS
2015 NL MVP, five-time
All-Star, 2015 NL
home run leader

Being the No. 1 pick of the MLB draft brings a ton of pressure. And in the case of these two, the expectations couldn't have been higher. Bryce Harper was just 16 years old when he landed on the cover of SPORTS ILLUSTRATED, hailed as the "chosen one." Griffey was a phenom whose father had the same name and an All-Star career. So both players had a lot to handle when they were still just teenagers. And yet, both became game-changing superstars almost immediately. Harper has a gorgeous lefthanded swing and smacked 22 home runs in his first season, when he was 19. Griffey also made his

KEN GRIFFEY JR.

Centerfielder

The OLD GUY

HEIGHT, WEIGHT
6'3", 195 pounds

TEAMS
Mariners, Reds, White Sox

CAREER STATS
AVG: .284 **HR**: 630 **RBI**: 1,836
RUNS: 1,662 **SB**: 184 (22 seasons)

AWARDS AND HONORS
1997 AL MVP, 13-time All-Star,
four-time AL home run leader
(1994, 1997–1999)

big league debut at age 19 and slugged 16 homers that season. His lefthanded swing was one of the sweetest the game has ever seen, and he sent pitch after pitch over the rightfield wall in Seattle's old Kingdome. Junior was responsible for bringing a little more fun to the game, flashing a big smile and often wearing his hat backward during batting practice. Harper has also made it his mission to bring joy to the game, and he even started a Make Baseball Fun Again campaign in 2016, hoping to encourage players to show a little more individuality on the field. His outgoing personality has been backed up by plenty of production on the field, as his first six seasons have put Harper on the path to becoming an all-time great.

GIANCARLO STANTON
Rightfielder

HEIGHT, WEIGHT
6' 6", 245 pounds

TEAMS
Marlins, Yankees

CAREER STATS
AVG: .268 **HR**: 267 **RBI**: 672
RUNS: 576 (eight seasons)

AWARDS AND HONORS
Four-time All-Star, two-time
NL home run leader (2014, 2017)

Who doesn't love watching really big guys hit really long home runs? That's the specialty of both these sluggers, who are among the largest and most physically intimidating players of their eras. Stanton, like Greenberg, battled injury early in his career, and he played his home games in one of the most pitcher-friendly stadiums in baseball. But as with Greenberg in the 1930s, no one can match Stanton's pure power: He led the NL in home runs twice before his 28th birthday. Greenberg's stats might not look eye-popping at first, but he likely would have joined the 500-home-run club had he not missed three full seasons—and parts of

HANK GREENBERG

First Baseman/Leftfielder

HEIGHT, WEIGHT
6'3", 210 pounds

TEAMS
Tigers, Pirates

CAREER STATS
AVG: .313 **HR**: 331 **RBI**: 1,274
RUNS: 1,046 (13 seasons)

AWARDS AND HONORS
Two-time AL MVP (1935, 1940), five-time All-Star, four-time AL home run leader (1935, 1938, 1940, 1946)

two others—while serving in World War II. After all, he topped 40 home runs in the full seasons before and after his service. (He also missed almost all of 1936 with a wrist injury.) When he hit 58 home runs in 1938, Greenberg tied the record for the second-most homers in MLB history. One other thing these two sluggers have in common: They swung big, and they picked up plenty of K's along the way. Greenberg led the AL in strikeouts in 1939. And over his first eight seasons in the big leagues, Stanton was one of only three players in the NL to have struck out 1,000 times.

The **CURRENT GUY**

KRIS BRYANT
Third Baseman

HEIGHT, WEIGHT
6'5", 230 pounds

TEAM
Cubs

CAREER STATS
AVG: .288 **HR**: 94 **RBI**: 274
RUNS: 319 (three seasons)

AWARDS AND HONORS
2016 NL MVP, two-time
All-Star (2015, 2016),
2016 World Series
champion

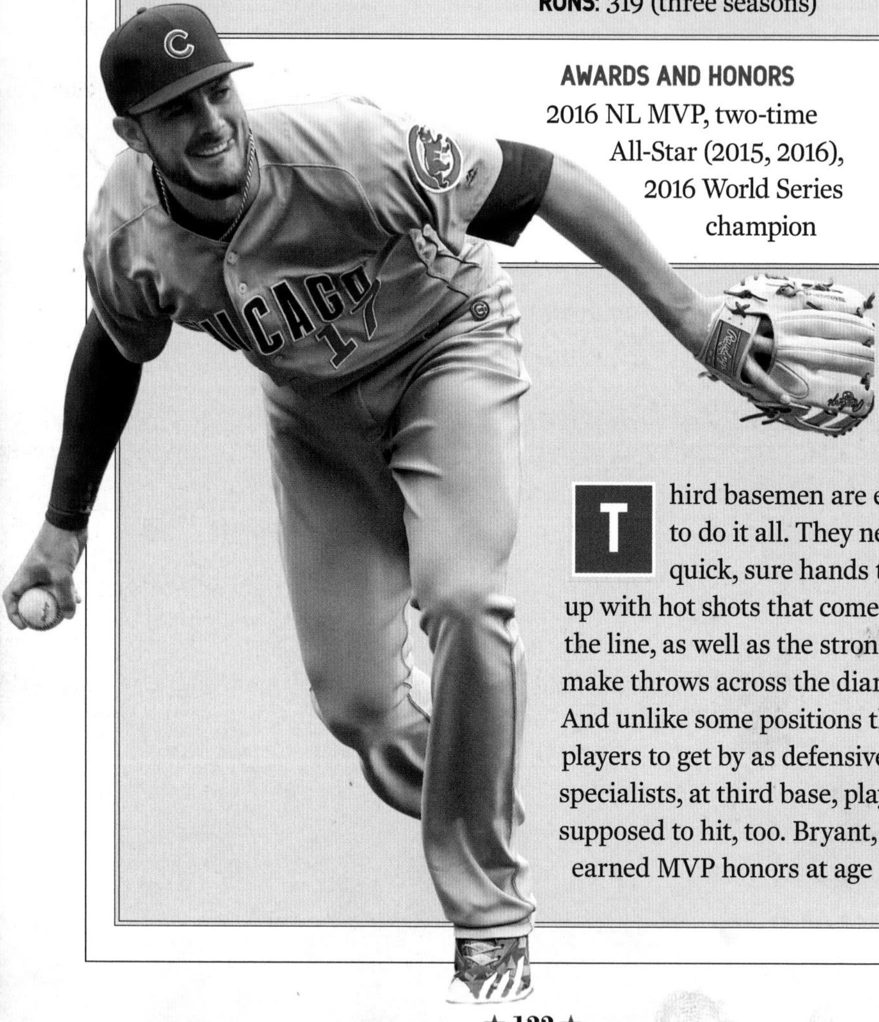

T hird basemen are expected to do it all. They need the quick, sure hands to come up with hot shots that come down the line, as well as the strong arms to make throws across the diamond. And unlike some positions that allow players to get by as defensive specialists, at third base, players are supposed to hit, too. Bryant, who earned MVP honors at age 24, is

MIKE SCHMIDT
Third Baseman

The OLD GUY

HEIGHT, WEIGHT
6' 2", 195 pounds

TEAM
Phillies

CAREER STATS
AVG: .267 **HR**: 548 **RBI**: 1,595
RUNS: 1,506 (18 seasons)

AWARDS AND HONORS
Three-time NL MVP (1980, 1981, 1986), 1980 World Series MVP, 12-time All-Star

shaping up to be the kind of phenom that Schmidt was—and no third baseman has ever hit as well as Schmidt. He consistently worked deep counts, which led to a lot of strikeouts but also a lot of walks. And when he made contact, it was usually hard contact. He led the NL in home runs in eight seasons, three between the ages of 24 and 26. Like Schmidt, Bryant does strike out a lot. (He had an NL-high 199 K's as a rookie in 2015 to go along with 26 home runs.) But there's no denying he's a similarly special offensive talent. Bryant has manned the hot corner for the Cubs, and his bat helped the team break its World Series drought in 2016.

MIGUEL CABRERA
Third Baseman/First Baseman

HEIGHT, WEIGHT
6' 4", 240 pounds

TEAMS
Marlins, Tigers

CAREER STATS
AVG: .317 **HR**: 462 **RBI**: 1,613
RUNS: 1,371 (15 seasons)

AWARDS AND HONORS
Two-time AL MVP (2012, 2013),
2012 AL Triple Crown winner,
11-time All-Star, four-time
AL batting champ

S ome excellent hitters crush pitches—but only when the ball is where they want it. Then there are hitters who cover so much of the plate that they can hammer anything in the vicinity of the strike zone. It's a rare trait seen only in baseball's truly elite hitters, and that's what Cabrera and Robinson, two sluggers who have starred in both leagues, brought to the table. Cabrera was traded from the NL to the AL while a superstar, part of a cost-cutting move by the Marlins.

FRANK ROBINSON
Outfielder/First Baseman

THE OLD GUY

HEIGHT, WEIGHT
6'1", 183 pounds

TEAMS
Reds, Orioles, Dodgers, Angels, Indians

CAREER STATS
AVG: .294 **HR**: 586 **RBI**: 1,812
RUNS: 1,829 (21 seasons)

AWARDS AND HONORS
Two-time MVP (1961, 1966), 1966 World Series MVP,
1966 AL Triple Crown winner, 14-time All-Star

And in 2012, the first of his back-to-back MVP seasons, he became the first player in 45 years to win a Triple Crown. In his prime he was impossible to pitch to because of his plate coverage; in 2011 he accomplished the rare feat of drawing more walks (108) than strikeouts (89). Robinson made a point of owning every part of the strike zone, crowding the plate and hammering outside pitches that others could only reach out and try to poke. He was traded from the Reds to the Orioles in his prime and won the Triple Crown in his first season with Baltimore, also becoming the only player to win MVP in both leagues.

JOEY VOTTO
First Baseman

HEIGHT, WEIGHT
6'2", 220 pounds

TEAM
Reds

CAREER STATS
AVG: .313 HR: 257 RBI: 830
RUNS: 863 (11 seasons)

AWARDS AND HONORS
2010 NL MVP,
five-time All-Star

The CURRENT GUY

O ccasionally, it takes time to realize just how impressive some of the great ones really were. Votto and Mize are two hitters who have been underappreciated. Votto has led the NL in on-base percentage six times, yet he has only made the All-Star Game five times. That's in part because of all the offensive stars in today's game and also because Votto's Cincinnati teams haven't won a playoff series in his career. Mize played during an era that included superstars Joe DiMaggio, Stan Musial, and Ted Williams, among others. At the time, there wasn't an emphasis on

JOHNNY MIZE
First Baseman

OLD GUY *The*

HEIGHT, WEIGHT
6' 2", 215 pounds

TEAMS
Cardinals, Giants, Yankees

CAREER STATS
AVG: .312 **HR**: 359 **RBI**: 1,337
RUNS: 1,118 (15 seasons)

AWARDS AND HONORS
10-time All-Star, 1939 NL
batting champion, four-time
NL home run leader

statistics like on-base percentage and OPS, stats that grew in popularity as managers and fans gained a greater understanding of the game. But Mize put up numbers that shouldn't be overlooked by anyone. The lefty-swinging first baseman posted an OBP above .400 in seven of his first eight big league seasons. He also led the National League in slugging percentage four times and OPS three times. Yet he was runner-up for MVP twice and didn't make it to the Hall of Fame until he was elected by the veteran's committee in 1981. He never got more than 43% of the required 75% of the baseball writers' vote to get in.

Chapter 6

TEAM TIDBITS

Learn a little something about each of the 30 MLB teams, from the biggest stars to the best seasons to every ballpark's dimensions.

ARIZONA DIAMONDBACKS NL WEST

FOUNDED

1998
Expansion franchise awarded to Arizona in 1995

THE GREATS

Luis Gonzalez, Outfielder He joined Arizona at age 31 and had five straight 100-RBI seasons (1999–2003). Gonzalez also hit 57 home runs in 2001.

Randy Johnson, Pitcher One of the most imposing hurlers ever, the 6'10" lefty won four consecutive Cy Young Awards with Arizona (1999–2002).

WORLD SERIES

**WINS: 1
LOSSES: 0**

Paul Goldschmidt, First Baseman Goldschmidt led the NL in homers (36) and RBIs (125) in 2013. One of baseball's top sluggers, he has been an MVP runner-up twice.

BEST SEASON

2001
92–70 regular-season record, World Series champions

Brandon Webb, Pitcher Armed with one of the best sinkers of all time, the righty won the 2006 NL Cy Young Award and led the league in wins in 2006 and 2008.

GOOD TO KNOW

Expansion teams are supposed to struggle, but the Diamondbacks won 100 games in 1999, just their second year. They fell short that postseason, but a World Series trophy wasn't far away. In 2001, Arizona faced off against the Yankees in one of the most exciting Fall Classics ever played. After forcing a Game 7, the D-Backs trailed 2–1 heading into the bottom of the ninth, with Yankees All-Star closer Mariano Rivera on the mound. Arizona scratched out two runs, capped by a bloop single from Luis Gonzalez *(near right)* that scored the Series-winning run. No expansion team won a title faster than the D-Backs, who won it all in their fourth season.

ATLANTA BRAVES

NL EAST

FOUNDED

1876
Originally Boston Red Stockings (1876–1882). Also Beaneaters (1883–1906), Doves (1907–1910), Rustlers (1911), Bees (1936–1940), Braves (1912–1935, 1941–1952). Then Milwaukee Braves. Moved to Atlanta in 1966

WORLD SERIES

**WINS: 3
LOSSES: 9**

BEST SEASON

1995
90–54 regular-season record, World Series champions

THE GREATS

Hank Aaron, Outfielder
Hammerin' Hank was baseball's all-time home run leader for more than 33 years after he retired in 1976. He's still first on the career RBI list (2,297).

Warren Spahn, Pitcher A 17-time All-Star for the Boston-Milwaukee Braves, Spahn was the second winner of the Cy Young Award, in 1957. He has more wins than any lefty in history (363).

Chipper Jones, Third Baseman He was the heart of the Braves' offense in the 1990s, winning National League MVP in 1999 and making eight All-Star teams.

John Smoltz, Pitcher An ace *and* a closer, Smoltz is the Braves' all-time leader in strikeouts (3,011), fifth in wins (210), and second in saves (154). He won the Cy Young Award in 1996.

GOOD TO KNOW

After averaging 100 losses per season from 1988 through 1990, the Braves launched one of the most impressive runs in sports history. They won 14 straight NL East titles from 1991 through 2005. No other team has won more than eight division titles in a row. Atlanta was powered by dominant pitching, with Greg Maddux *(second from left)* winning the NL Cy Young Award in each of his first three seasons in Atlanta (1993–1995) after signing as a free agent. Lefty Tom Glavine *(far left)* had two Cy Youngs and five 20-win seasons during that span, and John Smoltz *(second from right)* added a Cy Young as a starter in 1996, then later became Atlanta's closer and saved an NL-record 55 games in 2002.

BALTIMORE ORIOLES

AL EAST

FOUNDED

1901
Originally Milwaukee Brewers (1901). Also St. Louis Browns (1902–1953). Became Baltimore Orioles in 1954

WORLD SERIES

WINS: 3
LOSSES: 4

BEST SEASON

1970
108–54 regular-season record, World Series champions

THE GREATS

Cal Ripken Jr., Shortstop He's best known for playing in a record 2,632 consecutive games, but Ripken also earned two MVP Awards (1983, 1991).

Brooks Robinson, Third Baseman One of the finest defensive players in baseball history, Robinson was an 18-time All-Star, AL MVP in 1964, and World Series MVP in 1970.

Jim Palmer, Pitcher The righthander won three Cy Young Awards in the 1970s and was part of all three of Baltimore's World Series winners.

Eddie Murray, First Baseman The slugger led the majors in home runs (22) and RBIs (78) in the strike-shortened 1981 season. He finished in the top five in AL MVP voting every season from 1981 through 1985.

GOOD TO KNOW

In 1987, Orioles baseball was a family affair. One family, specifically. Cal Ripken Sr. *(center)* was the team's new skipper, and 26-year-old Cal Ripken Jr. *(far right)* was Baltimore's shortstop, a four-time All-Star who had already won AL MVP. That July, Ripken Jr. gained a new double-play partner: younger brother Billy *(near right)*, who joined the O's as a second baseman. On July 11, the Ripkens became the first family to have a father manage two of his sons in a major league game. The three often sat together on road trips. "We'd let Dad in on some of the secret things we had done as kids," Ripken Jr. said later. "But most of the time, we found that he knew about them all along."

BOSTON RED SOX AL EAST

FOUNDED

1901
Originally Boston Americans (1901–1907). Became Red Sox in 1908

WORLD SERIES

**WINS: 8
LOSSES: 5**

BEST SEASON

1912
105–47 regular-season record, World Series champions

THE GREATS

Ted Williams, Outfielder Arguably the best pure hitter ever, Williams was a six-time AL batting champ and four-time AL home run leader in the 1940s. He's the all-time leader in career on-base percentage (.482).

Carl Yastrzemski, Outfielder An 18-time All-Star, Yaz was best known for his 1967 season, when he won the batting Triple Crown.

David Ortiz, Designated Hitter Big Papi was one of baseball's greatest clutch hitters and part of three World Series winners in Boston (2004, 2007, 2013).

Cy Young, Pitcher While he played more seasons in Cleveland, Young's best years came in Boston; he led the major leagues in wins in each of his first three seasons with the Red Sox (1901 through 1903).

GOOD TO KNOW

Babe Ruth was a game-changer for the Red Sox, leading them to a World Series title in 1918 as a star hitter and pitcher. But after one more season in Boston, the Bambino was sold to the Yankees for cash. Granted, the $100,000 he was sold for was a lot of money in 1919; Red Sox owner Harry Frazee also got a loan of around $300,000 from the Yankees' owners. (The rumor was that Frazee needed the cash for his theater productions.) Ruth, of course, went on to become arguably the greatest hitter of all time while helping the Yankees become one of baseball's early dynasties. Meanwhile, the Sox went 86 years without a World Series title, a drought referred to as the Curse of the Bambino.

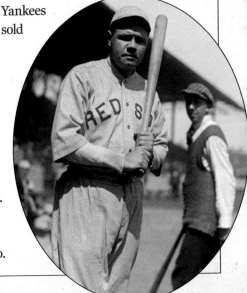

CHICAGO CUBS

NL CENTRAL

FOUNDED

1876

Originally Chicago White Stockings (1876–1889). Also Colts (1890–1897), Orphans (1898–1902). Became Cubs in 1903

WORLD SERIES

WINS: 3
LOSSES: 8

BEST SEASON

1907

107–45 regular-season record, World Series champions

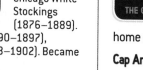

THE GREATS

Ernie Banks, First Baseman Known as Mr. Cub, Banks was NL MVP in 1958 and 1959 and one of two Cubs to slug 500 career home runs (512).

Cap Anson, First Baseman One of baseball's first true stars, Anson led the NL in RBIs eight times between 1880 and 1891.

Ron Santo, Third Baseman The Hall of Famer was an on-base machine who led the bigs in walks four times. He was also a slick defender and one of the most-loved Cubs ever. He announced Cubs games on the radio for 20 years, beginning in 1990.

Ryne Sandberg, Second Baseman Ryno led the NL in home runs in 1990 (40), one of four 40-homer seasons ever by a second baseman. The 10-time All-Star was also NL MVP in 1984.

GOOD TO KNOW

The Cubs have long embraced their reputation as Lovable Losers. And they've done a lot of losing: They went 108 years without a World Series title, and many pointed to the Curse of the Billy Goat. As the story goes, in 1945, William Sianis, owner of the Billy Goat Tavern and a pet goat named Murphy, was told he could no longer bring the goat into Wrigley Field for Cubs games because Murphy's smell was bothering fans. An incensed Sianis (whose nephew Sam, *near right*, and great-nephew Bill, *far right*, now own the Tavern) swore the Cubs wouldn't win anymore. That year the Cubs lost to the Tigers in the World Series. It took until 2016 for the Cubbies to get that long-awaited title.

CHICAGO WHITE SOX

AL CENTRAL

FOUNDED

1901
Originally
Chicago White
Stockings
(1900).
Became White Sox in 1901

WORLD SERIES

WINS: 3
LOSSES: 2

BEST SEASON

1917
99–54
regular-season
record,
World Series
champions

THE GREATS

Frank Thomas, First Baseman
The Big Hurt was a mammoth
6'5", 275-pound terror for
pitchers to face. He won
back-to-back AL MVP Awards in 1993 and 1994.

Luke Appling, Shortstop The slick-fielding Appling
won two AL batting titles (1936, 1943) in
his 20-year career, all of which he spent with
the White Sox.

Eddie Collins, Second Baseman He won an MVP with
the Philadelphia A's early in his career, in 1914,
but Collins went on to become the Sox' all-time
leader in stolen bases (368). He's also second in
franchise history in batting average (.331).

Nellie Fox, Second Baseman He made 11 straight
All-Star teams at one point; Fox took home AL MVP
honors in 1959 as well.

GOOD TO KNOW

Legend has it that Shoeless Joe Jackson earned his nickname
when he removed a new pair of cleats that were hurting his feet
and took an at bat in his socks. The
star outfielder was one of eight
players involved in the Black Sox scandal.
Upset with team owner Charles Comiskey
over pay, a group of players conspired
with gamblers to intentionally lose the
1919 World Series. The eight players
(Jackson and six others who allegedly
took money, plus another who knew
about the fix) were found not guilty in
court. But in 1921 commissioner
Kenesaw Mountain Landis banned
them from baseball. That penalty
remains in place and is the reason
Shoeless Joe is not in the Hall of Fame.

CINCINNATI REDS

NL CENTRAL

FOUNDED

1882
Originally Cincinnati Red Stockings (1882–1889). Became Reds in 1890 but were also Redlegs (1954–1958)

WORLD SERIES

WINS: 5
LOSSES: 4

BEST SEASON

1919
96–44 regular-season record, World Series champions

THE GREATS

Johnny Bench, Catcher The heart of the Big Red Machine, Bench was arguably the greatest catcher in history. The 14-time All-Star was NL MVP in 1970 and 1972, leading the NL in home runs both years.

Pete Rose, First Baseman–Outfielder Baseball's all-time hit king had 3,358 of his 4,256 career hits during his 19 seasons with the Reds. He was NL MVP in 1973 and World Series MVP in 1975.

Barry Larkin, Shortstop The Hall of Famer was one of the best-hitting shortstops of all time and spent each of his 19 MLB seasons in Cincinnati. Larkin was the 1995 NL MVP.

Frank Robinson, Outfielder He was NL MVP in 1961 and remains the only player to win the award in the NL and the AL. (He won with Baltimore in 1966.)

GOOD TO KNOW

The Reds had a disappointing 79–83 record in 1971, but a blockbuster trade changed everything: Cincinnati sent a package that included two All-Stars to the Astros. In exchange, the Reds got budding superstar second baseman Joe Morgan *(center)* and centerfielder César Gerónimo, who joined one of the greatest lineups of all time. With Morgan and fellow future Hall of Famers Johnny Bench *(far right)* and Tony Pérez, all-time hit king Pete Rose *(near right)*, and All-Stars Dave Concepción, George Foster, and Ken Griffey Sr., the Big Red Machine brought Cincinnati five NL West titles, three pennants, and back-to-back World Series wins (1975–1976) over the next eight seasons.

CLEVELAND INDIANS

 AL CENTRAL

1901
Originally Cleveland Blues (1901). Also Broncos (1902), Naps (1903–14). Became Indians in 1915

WINS: 2
LOSSES: 4

1920
98–56 regular-season record, World Series champions

THE GREATS

Bob Feller, Pitcher Armed with one of the best fastballs ever, Feller led the AL in strikeouts seven times and won the pitching Triple Crown in 1940.

Nap Lajoie, Second Baseman The reason that the team was called the Naps for 12 years (he was a player-manager for five seasons), Lajoie won four AL batting titles for Cleveland in the early 20th century. He hit .300 in 10 seasons.

Tris Speaker, Outfielder One of the greatest defensive outfielders of all time, Speaker won the AL batting title in 1916 and led the league in RBIs in 1923.

Lou Boudreau, Shortstop He won AL MVP in 1948, when he led Cleveland to its most recent World Series victory.

GOOD TO KNOW

That rumble you hear at Indians home games isn't thunder. It's the drummer, Cleveland superfan John Adams. In the old Cleveland Stadium, fans used to bang their folding seats to make noise during big moments. Adams preferred to sit in the bleachers, where there were no folding seats. So in 1973, when he was 21 years old, Adams went to the game with a bass drum and a couple of mallets to make noise. Fellow fans loved it, and so did the team. The Indians awarded Adams two season tickets—one for him, one for his drum. At the end of the 2016 season, Adams told the Cleveland *Plain Dealer* that he had only missed about 40 home games in 43 seasons.

COLORADO ROCKIES NL WEST

FOUNDED

1993
Expansion franchise awarded to Colorado in 1991

THE GREATS

Todd Helton, First Baseman Colorado's all-time leader in hits (2,519) and homers (369), Helton led the majors in batting average (.372) and RBIs (147) in 2000.

Larry Walker, Outfielder In his 10 seasons with the Rockies, Walker won three NL batting titles and led the league in home runs (49) during his MVP season in 1997.

WORLD SERIES

**WINS: 0
LOSSES: 1**

Troy Tulowitzki, Shortstop Tulowitzki's 10 seasons in Colorado included five All-Star appearances and two Silver Slugger Awards (2010, 2011).

BEST SEASON

2007
90–73 regular-season record, National League champions

Matt Holliday, Outfielder He played only five seasons with the Rockies but made three All-Star appearances. In 2007 he led the NL in batting average (.340) and RBIs (137) while also winning MVP of the NLCS.

GOOD TO KNOW

As the saying goes, "It's never over at Coors Field." That's because since the Rockies played their first game, in 1993, there have been more runs scored in Colorado (12.1 per game) than in any other big league city. Much of it has to do with the thin air in the high altitude of Denver, which makes the ball travel farther. Coors Field also has extra-deep walls, which limits homers but makes it easier to drop in base hits. All that offense leads to plenty of late-inning drama, like the wild-card tiebreaker in 2007. After the Padres scored twice in the top of the 13th inning, the Rockies scored three runs. Matt Holliday *(far right)* tripled home the tying run, then scored on a sacrifice fly to win it. Three weeks later the Rockies were in the World Series for the first time.

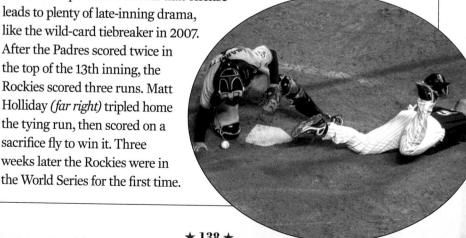

DETROIT TIGERS

AL CENTRAL

1901
One of four American League teams playing in the city in which they were founded

WINS: 4
LOSSES: 7

1984
104–58 regular-season record, World Series champions

THE GREATS

Ty Cobb, Outfielder His career .366 average still stands as the best of all time. Cobb collected 12 AL batting titles in his 22 seasons in Detroit and was the 1911 AL MVP.

Al Kaline, Outfielder Kaline's 22 Hall of Fame seasons with the Tigers were highlighted by 18 All-Star appearances, the 1955 AL batting title (.340), and a World Series championship in 1968.

Miguel Cabrera, First Baseman Acquired from the Marlins in 2007, Cabrera won back-to-back AL MVPs in 2012 (when he became the first player in 45 years to win the batting Triple Crown) and 2013.

Hank Greenberg, First Baseman A two-time AL MVP (1935, 1940), Greenberg led the league in home runs and RBIs four times apiece.

GOOD TO KNOW

When George (Sparky) Anderson was hired as manager in June 1979, the Tigers were on their way to missing a seventh straight postseason. Anderson said his Tigers had enough young talent to win a pennant in the next five years. Few believed him. But led by homegrown stars such as Alan Trammell, Lou Whitaker, and Kirk Gibson, Detroit returned to the playoffs in 1984, sweeping the Royals in the ALCS and beating the Padres in five games to win the World Series. The team's slogan—Bless you, boys—was inspired by local sportscaster Al Ackerman, who used it sarcastically after a win by the struggling Tigers. The phrase took on new meaning as the team moved toward a world championship.

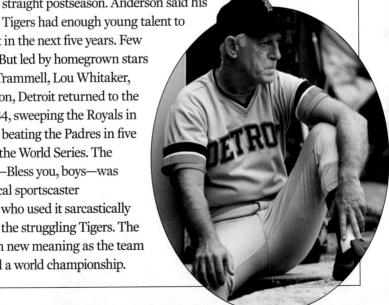

HOUSTON ASTROS

AL WEST

FOUNDED

1962
Originally Houston Colt .45s (1962–1964). Became Astros in 1965

WORLD SERIES

WINS: 1
LOSSES: 1

BEST SEASON

2017
101–61 regular-season record, World Series champions

THE GREATS

Jeff Bagwell, First Baseman Despite playing many home games in the pitcher-friendly Astrodome, the Hall of Famer slugged 449 career homers, the most in team history, and was NL MVP in 1994.

Craig Biggio, Second Baseman Playing all 20 of his MLB seasons in Houston, the Hall of Famer made seven All-Star teams and twice led the majors in runs scored (1995, 1997).

Roy Oswalt, Pitcher Houston's ace during the 2000s, Oswalt finished in the top five in NL Cy Young voting five times during a six-year span (2001–2006).

Lance Berkman, Outfielder This switch-hitting slugger was one of 10 players to hit 300 home runs during the first decade of the 2000s.

GOOD TO KNOW

Major League Baseball came to Houston in 1962, with one problem: It was hot and humid. The plan to beat the heat? The first indoor stadium. Known as the Colt .45s for the first three seasons, the team played outdoors at Colt Stadium. But in 1965 the team changed its name to the Astros in honor of its futuristic new stadium, the Astrodome (named for NASA's manned space program, headquartered in Houston). The stadium was a marvel, earning the nickname the Eighth Wonder of the World, and it soon paved the way for more new tech. After the grass died quickly during the 1965 season, the team installed artificial grass, known as AstroTurf, in the dome.

KANSAS CITY ROYALS AL CENTRAL

1969
Expansion franchise awarded to Kansas City in 1968

George Brett, Third Baseman
A 13-time All-Star who spent his entire 21-year career in K.C., Brett won three AL batting titles, including when he had a .390 average in 1980.

Bret Saberhagen, Pitcher The righthander's eight seasons with the Royals included Cy Young Awards in 1985 and 1989.

WINS: 2
LOSSES: 2

Dan Quisenberry, Pitcher Dominating with an unusual submarine-style delivery, Quisenberry led the AL in saves five times in the 1980s. He finished in the top 10 in MVP voting four times.

2015
95–67 regular-season record, World Series champions

Frank White, Second Baseman A cornerstone in Kansas City for 18 seasons, White was a rock defensively who made five All-Star teams. He was ALCS MVP in 1980 and helped the Royals to a World Series win in 1985.

On July 24, 1983, George Brett slugged a two-out, two-run, go-ahead homer in the top of the ninth at Yankee Stadium. After Brett touched home, New York manager Billy Martin asked that Brett's bat be examined for too much pine tar. The umpires agreed. After being called out to end the game, an enraged Brett charged out of the dugout, shouting. AL president Lee MacPhail later upheld the Royals' protest. (The MLB rulebook says a bat can't have more than 18 inches of pine tar on it, but the rule is meant to keep baseballs clean.) The matchup resumed in August, with the Royals in the lead. Brett, who had been ejected from the game, didn't come to the stadium. K.C. finished off the win.

LOS ANGELES ANGELS

AL WEST

1961
Originally
Los Angeles
Angels
(1961–1964).
Also California Angels (1965–1996),
Anaheim Angels (1997–2004),
Los Angeles Angels of Anaheim
(2005–2016)

WINS: 1
LOSSES: 0

2002
99–63
regular-season
record,
World Series
champions

Nolan Ryan, Pitcher
He emerged as a star after joining
the Angels in 1972, leading the
majors in strikeouts in seven of
the eight seasons he played in California.

Jim Fregosi, Shortstop A six-time All-Star during the
1960s, Fregosi went on to manage the Angels for
four seasons.

Mike Trout, Outfielder Seven seasons into his
career, Trout was already established as an
Angels great. A superstar at the plate and in
centerfield, he won AL Rookie of the Year in 2012
and AL MVP in 2014 and 2016.

Chuck Finley, Pitcher The big lefty was a workhorse
in the Angels' rotation during the late 1980s and
1990s, making four All-Star teams in 14 seasons
with the team.

During a June 2000 game, the Angels were trailing the Giants
5–4 heading into the bottom of the ninth, when scoreboard
operators debuted a new video. They
took a clip of a jumping monkey
(from the 1994 Jim Carrey comedy *Ace
Ventura: Pet Detective*) and proclaimed it the
Rally Monkey. Sure enough, the Angels
came back to win. The Rally Monkey
became a star—and shone during the
2002 World Series. With the Angels
trying to fend off elimination in Game 6
(against the Giants, again), they trailed
5–0 heading into the bottom of the
seventh inning when the Rally Monkey
made his appearance. The Angels
mounted a comeback, winning 6–5, then
taking the World Series in seven games.

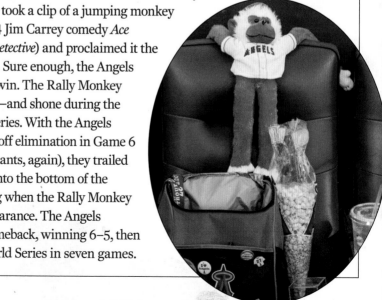

LOS ANGELES DODGERS

NL WEST

FOUNDED

1884

Originally Brooklyn Atlantics (1884). Also Grays (1885–1887), Bridegrooms (1888–1890, 1896–1898), Grooms (1891–1895); Superbas (1899–1910, 1913), Robins (1914–1931), and Dodgers (1911–12, 1932–1957). Moved to L.A. in 1958

WORLD SERIES

WINS: 6
LOSSES: 13

BEST SEASON

1955

98–55 regular-season record, World Series champions

THE GREATS

Jackie Robinson, Second Baseman Most famous for being the first African-American player in the majors, Robinson was a superstar talent: He won NL MVP in 1949 and helped Brooklyn to a World Series win in 1955.

Sandy Koufax, Pitcher Injuries cut his career short, but the lefty still managed three Cy Young Awards, an NL MVP in 1963, and two World Series MVPs over 12 seasons.

Duke Snider, Outfielder Hitting in the heart of Brooklyn's lineup, the Hall of Famer smacked 40 or more homers in five straight seasons from 1953 through 1957.

Clayton Kershaw, Pitcher Before turning 30, Kershaw had already picked up three Cy Young Awards (2011, 2013, 2014) and won NL MVP (2014).

GOOD TO KNOW

Jackie Robinson showed great courage while breaking Major League Baseball's color barrier in 1947. He was constantly the subject of abuse from fans, opponents, and even teammates. But he had friends in the Dodgers' infield: Second baseman Eddie Stanky often defended Robinson *(below, left)* against racial taunts. Then there was Harold (Pee Wee) Reese *(below, right)*, the Dodgers' team captain. Reese admitted that he had never shaken hands with a black person before he met his teammate. Seventy years after Robinson made his debut, the team unveiled a statue of him outside Dodger Stadium in L.A. The monument depicts Robinson stealing home, which he did an impressive 19 times in his career.

MIAMI MARLINS NL EAST

FOUNDED

1993
Originally Florida Marlins (1993–2011). Became Miami Marlins in 2012

WORLD SERIES

WINS: 2
LOSSES: 0

BEST SEASON

1997
92–70 regular-season record, World Series champions

THE GREATS

Hanley Ramírez, Shortstop One of baseball's top-hitting shortstops during his seven seasons in Miami, Ramírez was a three-time All-Star and won the NL batting title (.342) in 2009.

Luis Castillo, Second Baseman An on-base machine, Castillo made three All-Star teams and twice led the majors in stolen bases (2000, 2002) during his time with the Marlins.

Jeff Conine, First Baseman—Outfielder Mr. Marlin was traded after the team's 1997 World Series title, then was traded back in time to help the Marlins win the 2003 championship.

Giancarlo Stanton, Outfielder Known for his mammoth home runs, Stanton made three All-Star Games in his first six seasons and led the NL in home runs in 2014 (37) and 2017 (59).

GOOD TO KNOW

The Marlins shocked the baseball world in 1997, winning a World Series in just their fifth season in existence. But owner Wayne Huizenga said the team was losing money, so he traded away most of the stars. By the beginning of 1999, the club had the lowest payroll in baseball; the Marlins were starting from scratch again. And yet, after five straight losing seasons, the team was right back in the World Series in 2003. Led by young aces Josh Beckett *(center)* and Dontrelle Willis, speedsters Juan Pierre and Luis Castillo, star catcher Iván Rodríguez, and 20-year-old slugger Miguel Cabrera, the Marlins won 91 games and clinched a second World Series title, at Yankee Stadium.

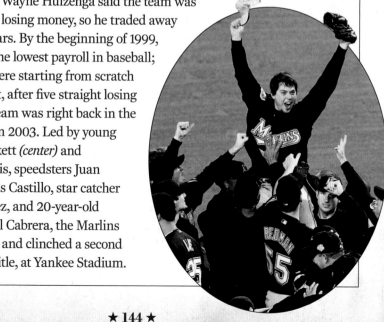

MILWAUKEE BREWERS

NL CENTRAL

FOUNDED

1969
Originally
Seattle Pilots
(1969).
Became
Milwaukee Brewers in 1970

WORLD SERIES

WINS: 0
LOSSES: 1

BEST SEASON

1982
95–67
regular-season
record,
American League
champions

THE GREATS

Robin Yount, Shortstop The AL MVP in 1982 and 1989, Yount is the Brewers' all-time leader in numerous categories, including hits (3,142) and RBIs (1,406).

Paul Molitor, Third Baseman A line-drive machine, Molitor made five All-Star teams and led the AL in runs scored three times (1982, 1987, 1991) during his 15 years in Milwaukee.

Ryan Braun, Outfielder Braun burst onto the scene in 2007, winning NL Rookie of the Year. He won NL MVP in 2011 and led the league in homers in 2012 (41).

Cecil Cooper, First Baseman Acquired from Boston in 1976, Cooper went on to make five All-Star teams. He led the AL in RBIs twice during his 11 seasons with the Brewers.

GOOD TO KNOW

Originally, the Royals and the Seattle Pilots were set to enter MLB in 1971, but Kansas City wanted to move the timeline up by two years. The Pilots weren't ready, and the team went bankrupt after the 1969 season. Bud Selig bought the Pilots with the intention of moving them to Milwaukee. The move wasn't finalized until six days before Opening Day in 1970! The team, renamed the Brewers, didn't have enough time to get new uniforms, so they actually took the Pilots' uniforms, removed the name, and re-stitched them with BREWERS. The team still wore the Pilots' unique piping on the sleeves, and if you looked closely, you could see the outline of the old logo on the jerseys.

MINNESOTA TWINS

AL CENTRAL

FOUNDED

1901
Originally Washington Senators (1901–60). Became Minnesota Twins in 1961

THE GREATS

Rod Carew, First Baseman An All-Star in each of his 12 seasons with the Twins, Carew won seven AL batting titles, including when he hit .388 and won AL MVP in 1977.

Walter Johnson, Pitcher Playing for the Senators, the Big Train dominated with an unhittable fastball, winning AL MVP twice (1913, 1924).

WORLD SERIES

WINS: 3
LOSSES: 3

Kirby Puckett, Outfielder He wasn't built like a baseball superstar (5'8", 210 pounds), but Puckett was a 10-time All-Star and the heart of two World Series winners (1987, 1991).

BEST SEASON

1991
95–67 regular-season record, World Series champions

Harmon Killebrew, First Baseman One of the top power hitters of the 1960s, Killebrew led the AL in home runs six times and won league MVP in 1969.

GOOD TO KNOW

Many consider the 1991 World Series to be the greatest in baseball history. Game 7 of that Series, played at Minnesota's Metrodome, was an all-time classic. Twins ace Jack Morris *(right)* pitched 10 shutout innings. Atlanta's John Smoltz combined with two relievers to throw nine shutout innings. Braves ace reliever Alejandro Peña allowed a broken-bat, bloop double to Dan Gladden to start the bottom of the 10th. A sacrifice bunt, followed by intentional walks to Twins stars Kirby Puckett and Kent Hrbek, left the bases loaded with one out for pinch hitter Gene Larkin. The veteran punched a deep fly ball over the drawn-in outfield; the walk-off hit scored the game's only run.

NEW YORK METS

NL EAST

1962
Expansion franchise awarded to New York in 1961

WINS: 2
LOSSES: 3

1986
108–54 regular-season record, World Series champions

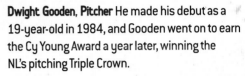

Tom Seaver, Pitcher
Tom Terrific won three Cy Young Awards with the Mets and helped pitch them to a World Series championship in 1969.

Dwight Gooden, Pitcher He made his debut as a 19-year-old in 1984, and Gooden went on to earn the Cy Young Award a year later, winning the NL's pitching Triple Crown.

David Wright, Third Baseman Before back injuries limited him, Wright made seven All-Star teams in an eight-year span and won two Silver Slugger Awards (2007, 2008).

Darryl Strawberry, Outfielder He played only eight seasons with the Mets, starting with his Rookie of the Year effort in 1983, but Strawberry slugged 252 homers in that time and made seven All-Star teams.

Over their first seven seasons, the Mets lost 100 games five times and never came within 24 games of the playoffs. It looked as if 1969 would be just as unmemorable—the Mets began with an 18–23 record. But they went on an 11-game winning streak and posted a .678 winning percentage over the rest of the season, making the World Series with great pitching and defense. Behind aces Tom Seaver and Jerry Koosman, strong pitching from Gary Gentry and Nolan Ryan in Game 3, and a couple of stupendous catches by centerfielder Tommie Agee (*far right*, with Jerry Grote), the Miracle Mets finished off the favored Orioles in five games to complete the incredible turnaround.

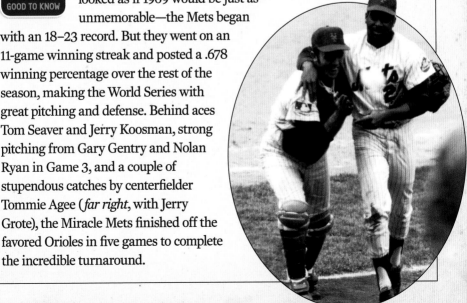

NEW YORK YANKEES

AL EAST

1903
Originally
New York
Highlanders
(1903–1912).
Became
Yankees in 1913

WINS: 27
LOSSES: 13

1927
110–44
regular-season
record,
World Series
champions

Babe Ruth, Outfielder The most dominant hitter of all time, Ruth joined the Yankees in 1920 and went on to lead the AL in homers 10 times in 15 seasons.

Lou Gehrig, First Baseman The Iron Horse played in 2,130 consecutive games before amyotrophic lateral sclerosis (ALS) ended his career. The Yankees' captain won two AL MVP Awards (1927, 1936) and six World Series rings.

Mickey Mantle, Outfielder This larger-than-life dynamo won three MVP Awards (1956, 1957, 1962) while helping the Yanks win seven World Series.

Joe DiMaggio, Outfielder Best known for his record 56-game hitting streak in 1941, Joltin' Joe won three AL MVPs (1939, 1941, 1947) and led the Yankees to nine World Series titles.

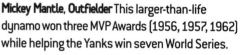

Nearly a century later, the 1927 Yankees still stand as baseball's best team. They won more games than any World Series champion in the 154-game era, then swept Pittsburgh in the Fall Classic. Babe Ruth *(far right)* slugged a then-MLB-record 60 home runs but didn't even win AL MVP. That honor went to Lou Gehrig *(near right)*, who had a league-leading 173 RBIs while hitting .373 with 47 homers. Ruth, second baseman Tony Lazzeri, and leftfielder Bob Meusel all drove in more than 100 runs. Centerfielder Earle Combs hit .356. There were four future Hall of Famers in the everyday lineup (Ruth, Gehrig, Lazzeri, and Combs), and two on the pitching staff (Herb Pennock and Waite Hoyt).

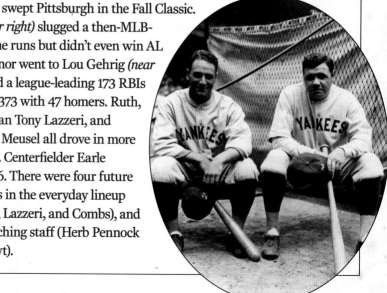

OAKLAND ATHLETICS AL WEST

FOUNDED

1901

Originally Philadelphia Athletics (1901–1954). Also Kansas City Athletics (1955–1967). Moved to Oakland in 1968

WORLD SERIES

WINS: 9
LOSSES: 6

BEST SEASON

1929

104–46 regular-season record, World Series champions

THE GREATS

Rickey Henderson, Outfielder The greatest leadoff hitter in history, Henderson played 14 seasons in Oakland, topping 100 stolen bases in a year three times and winning AL MVP in 1990.

Jimmie Foxx, First Baseman The slugger won two AL MVP Awards (1932, 1933) in 11 seasons with the team and led the league in home runs three times.

Lefty Grove, Pitcher In his nine seasons with the Philadelphia A's in the 1920s and 1930s, the southpaw led the AL in strikeouts seven times, ERA five times, and wins four times.

Eddie Plank, Pitcher He threw more shutouts (69) than any other lefthanded pitcher in history and helped the Philadelphia A's to two World Series titles (1911, 1913).

GOOD TO KNOW

It's not often a team that never even played for a championship inspires a best-selling book and a blockbuster movie. The Oakland A's of the early 2000s did just that as the source of the story for *Moneyball.* In the 1990s big-market teams held a significant advantage over small-market teams; the Yankees, for example, could afford big-money free agents that other teams couldn't. A's GM Billy Beane (played by Brad Pitt, *right*, in the movie) built the small-market A's a different way, finding valuable players who had been passed over by other teams due to underwhelming traditional statistics. Despite their low payroll, the A's went to the playoffs four straight seasons, from 2000 through 2003.

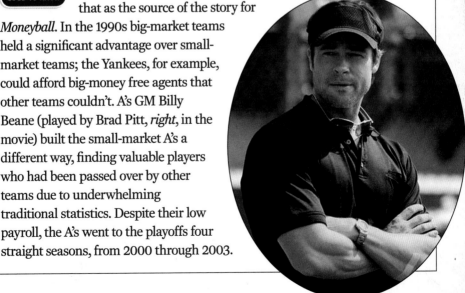

PHILADELPHIA PHILLIES

NL EAST

FOUNDED

1883
Originally Philadelphia Quakers (1883–1889). Became Phillies in 1890

WORLD SERIES

WINS: 2
LOSSES: 5

BEST SEASON

2008
92–70 regular-season record, World Series champions

THE GREATS

Mike Schmidt, Third Baseman Schmidt won three NL MVP Awards, led the league in home runs eight times, and won MVP of the 1980 World Series, the Phillies' first title.

Robin Roberts, Pitcher The Hall of Fame righthander led the majors in wins four straight times (1952–1955) and in strikeouts in back-to-back seasons (1953–1954).

Steve Carlton, Pitcher Armed with an unhittable slider, Carlton joined Philly in 1972 and won the pitching Triple Crown and the first of four Cy Young Awards.

Chase Utley, Second Baseman The hard-nosed Utley was one of the best offensive middle infielders of the modern era, winning four Silver Slugger Awards (2006–2009).

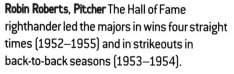

GOOD TO KNOW

The 1993 Phillies were a surprising success story, going from worst to first in the NL East; they won 97 games during the regular season and the pennant.

Philadelphia was a talented team overflowing with big personalities and lots of mullets and facial hair. No one embodied the team's unique personality more than first baseman John Kruk, who sported long hair and a scruffy beard, hit .316, and made his third All-Star Game that season. The Phillies' misfits made it to the World Series but lost to the Blue Jays in six games, when closer Mitch (Wild Thing) Williams allowed a three-run walk-off homer to Joe Carter to end the season.

PITTSBURGH PIRATES

NL CENTRAL

FOUNDED

1882
Originally Pittsburgh Alleghenys (1882–1990). Became Pirates in 1891

WORLD SERIES

WINS: 5
LOSSES: 4

BEST SEASON

1909
110–42 regular-season record, World Series champions

THE GREATS

Roberto Clemente, Outfielder Baseball's first Latin American star, Clemente played all 18 of his MLB seasons with the Pirates, winning NL MVP in 1966, World Series MVP in 1971, and collecting 3,000 hits.

Honus Wagner, Shortstop Considered the greatest player of baseball's Dead Ball era, Wagner won eight NL batting titles in 18 years with the Pirates in the early 20th century.

Paul Waner, Outfielder Waner hit .340 over his 15 seasons in Pittsburgh, including .380 during his NL MVP season in 1927.

Arky Vaughan, Shortstop This Hall of Famer played 10 seasons with the Pirates, making the All-Star team eight times and winning the NL batting title (.385) in 1935.

GOOD TO KNOW

As famous as he was for playing baseball, Roberto Clemente was nearly as well-known for his humanitarian efforts. An earthquake devastated Managua, the capital of Nicaragua, in December 1972, just weeks after he visited. He arranged for relief packages to be delivered three times in the days after the quake, but corrupt Nicaraguan officials diverted them. Clemente decided to accompany a fourth delivery to ensure it got to those who needed it. But his flight, on New Year's Eve, crashed into the ocean soon after takeoff, and Clemente was never found. He died a hero on and off the field, and in 1973, in a special election, he was the first Latin American player enshrined in the Baseball Hall of Fame.

ST. LOUIS CARDINALS

NL CENTRAL

1882
Originally St. Louis Brown Stockings (1882). Also Browns (1883–1998), Perfectos (1899). Became Cardinals in 1900

FOUNDED

WINS: 11
LOSSES: 8

WORLD SERIES

1942
106–48 regular-season record, World Series champions

BEST SEASON

THE GREATS

Stan Musial, Outfielder Stan the Man won three National League MVP Awards in the 1940s while leading the Cards to three World Series championships.

Rogers Hornsby, Second Baseman His .424 average in 1924 remains an NL record, and Hornsby won the league batting Triple Crown twice during his 13 seasons with the franchise.

Bob Gibson, Pitcher Known for his fierce competitiveness, the righthander's 1.12 ERA in 1968 was (and still is) the lowest since 1914 and earned him league MVP and the first of two NL Cy Young Awards.

Albert Pujols, First Baseman His 11 seasons in St. Louis included three NL MVP Awards (2005, 2008, 2009) and two World Series (2006, 2011).

GOOD TO KNOW

Usually you have to hammer homers or rack up hits to become famous. Not so with Ozzie Smith. He was a good offensive player, but defense made him a household name. Known as the Wizard of Oz, Smith was amazingly athletic and nimble; he would jog onto the field and perform backflips before games. He played his first four seasons in San Diego before being traded to St. Louis, where he played for 15 years (1982–1996). He made spectacular, diving plays. As Mets shortstop Bud Harrelson once said, "The thing about Ozzie is, if he misses a ball, you assume it's uncatchable. If any other shortstop misses a ball, your first thought is, 'Would Ozzie have had it?'"

SAN DIEGO PADRES

NL WEST

FOUNDED

1969
Expansion franchise awarded to San Diego in 1968

THE GREATS

Tony Gwynn, Outfielder Known as Mr. Padre, Gwynn was a hitting machine who won eight NL batting titles in the 1980s and 1990s. He spent his entire 20-year career in San Diego.

Dave Winfield, Outfielder A college basketball star who was also drafted by the NFL's Minnesota Vikings, the 6'6" Winfield was a big presence in the Padres' lineup during the 1970s. He led the NL in RBIs in 1979 (118).

WORLD SERIES

**WINS: 0
LOSSES: 2**

Trevor Hoffman, Pitcher The NL's all-time saves leader (601), Hoffman saved 30 or more games in 14 seasons for the Padres in the 1990s and 2000s.

BEST SEASON

1998
98–64 regular-season record, National League champions

Jake Peavy, Pitcher Peavy led the majors in ERA twice (2004, 2007) and earned the NL Cy Young Award in 2007, when he won the pitching Triple Crown.

GOOD TO KNOW

The Padres' biggest star in the 1970s and 1980s was either Hall of Fame hit machine Tony Gwynn—or a guy in a giant chicken suit. Originally a mascot for a local radio station, the Chicken became a regular at San Diego's Jack Murphy Stadium, appearing at more than 500 games in a row at one point and often drawing just as much attention as the game on the field. In 1979 the radio station fired the man inside, Ted Giannoulas, and replaced him, but fans found out and started booing the new chicken. That summer, Giannoulas designed his own costume and was eventually allowed back. The Chicken went on to star in a TV show, *The Baseball Bunch*, and even had his own baseball card.

SAN FRANCISCO GIANTS

NL WEST

FOUNDED

1883
Originally New York Gothams (1883–1884). Also New York Giants (1885–1957). Moved to San Francisco in 1958

WORLD SERIES

WINS: 6
LOSSES: 15

BEST SEASON

1905
105–48 regular-season record, World Series champions

THE GREATS

Willie Mays, Outfielder One of the best all-around players in baseball history, Mays won NL MVP in 1954 and 1965, led the league in home runs and stolen bases four times apiece, and won the batting title in 1954.

Mel Ott, Outfielder Ott led the NL in home runs six times during the 1930s and 1940s.

Christy Mathewson, Pitcher The New York Giants' ace led the NL in ERA five times, wins four times, and strikeouts five times between 1903 and 1913.

Barry Bonds, Outfielder His reputation is marred by alleged steroid use, but Bonds's performance over 15 seasons with the Giants (.477 on-base percentage, 586 home runs including a record 73 in 2001, five NL MVP Awards) is unmatched in baseball history.

GOOD TO KNOW

In the 1954 World Series, the Giants and the Indians entered the eighth inning of Game 1 with the score tied 2–2. With men on first and second, Cleveland's Vic Wertz blasted a ball to center. The Polo Grounds, where the Giants played, was unusually shaped and had an especially deep centerfield wall. Mays sprinted back and made an over-the-shoulder grab with his back to home plate, around 420 feet away. He then winged an incredible throw to the infield, keeping the man on second from scoring after tagging up. The play is now simply known as the Catch. The Giants escaped the inning without allowing a run, won Game 1 in extra innings, and swept the Indians to win the title.

SEATTLE MARINERS

AL WEST

FOUNDED

1977
Seattle was awarded an expansion franchise as part of a settlement with AL after Seattle Pilots relocation

WORLD SERIES

WINS: 0
LOSSES: 0

BEST SEASON

2001
116–46 regular-season record, American League West champions

THE GREATS

Ken Griffey Jr., Outfielder Junior was known for his sweet swing and acrobatic catches in centerfield. He was AL MVP in 1997 and an All-Star in 10 straight seasons for Seattle (1990–1999).

Ichiro Suzuki, Outfielder If you combine this superstar's big league hits with the 1,278 he had in Japan, he has more than anyone in MLB history.

Edgar Martinez, Designated Hitter A seven-time All-Star in the 1990s and early 2000s, Martinez is Seattle's all-time leader in RBIs (1,261) and is second in hits (2,247) and home runs (309).

Felix Hernandez, Pitcher Seattle's ace since breaking into the majors at age 19, King Felix won the AL Cy Young Award in 2010 and has led the league in ERA twice (2010, 2014).

GOOD TO KNOW

By the start of the 21st century, baseball had already seen a handful of star pitchers make the move from Japan and find success in the majors. But when 5'10", 170-pound Ichiro Suzuki came to the U.S., some were skeptical because the outfielder didn't look like the muscled-up sluggers dominating MLB at the time. But he turned out to be a game-changing talent, a speedster with phenomenal bat skills. In 2001 he became the second player to win Rookie of the Year and MVP in the same season, leading Seattle to 116 wins, tied for most ever. He made the All-Star Game in each of his first 10 seasons and surpassed 3,000 hits despite not making his MLB debut until age 27.

TAMPA BAY RAYS

AL EAST

FOUNDED

1998
Originally
Tampa Bay
Devil Rays
(1998–2007).
Became Rays in 2008

WORLD SERIES

**WINS: 0
LOSSES: 1**

BEST SEASON

2008
97–65
regular-season
record,
American League
champions

THE GREATS

Evan Longoria, Third Baseman
Along with having racked up some of the biggest hits in Rays history, Longoria is a three-time All-Star and was the 2008 AL Rookie of the Year.

Carl Crawford, Outfielder The speedy outfielder made four All-Star teams and led the AL in stolen bases four times during the 2000s.

Ben Zobrist, Infielder–Outfielder While playing just about every position on the diamond for nine seasons with the Rays, Zobrist's versatility and ability to get on base earned him spots on two All-Star teams (2009, 2013).

David Price, Pitcher The lefty won the AL Cy Young Award in 2012, when he led the league with 20 wins, and was the runner-up in 2010. He also made four All-Star teams while with the Rays.

GOOD TO KNOW

The Rays and the Red Sox entered the final day of the 2011 season tied for the AL wild-card spot. Things weren't looking good for the Rays that night: The Sox led the Orioles 3–2 entering the ninth, while Tampa Bay trailed the Yankees 7–0 in the eighth. But the Rays rallied, scoring six runs that inning. Then, with two outs in the bottom of the ninth, Dan Johnson smacked an unlikely home run to tie it. In Baltimore, the Orioles scored twice off Boston closer Jonathan Papelbon to win shortly after midnight. Three minutes later, in the 12th inning in Florida, Evan Longoria lined a walk-off homer, sending the Rays to the playoffs and finishing the most exciting night in baseball history.

TEXAS RANGERS

AL WEST

1961
Originally Washington Senators (1961–1971). Became Texas Rangers in 1972

WINS: 0
LOSSES: 2

2011
96–66 regular-season record, American League champions

THE GREATS

Iván Rodríguez, Catcher Known for his ability to throw out base runners, Pudge also hit .304 over his 13 seasons in Texas and won American League MVP in 1999.

Frank Howard, Outfielder Nicknamed the Capitol Punisher for his time smashing long home runs for the Washington Senators, the 6'7", 255-pound Howard led the AL in home runs in 1968 and 1970 (44 in each season) and hit a career-high 48 in 1969.

Juan Gonzalez, Outfielder Gonzalez won AL MVP in 1996 and 1998 while smacking five 40-homer seasons during the 1990s.

Michael Young, Infielder A seven-time All-Star, Young twice led the AL in hits (2005 and 2013) and won the AL batting title (.331) in 2005.

GOOD TO KNOW

Only 31 pitchers have thrown multiple no-hitters in the majors. Nolan Ryan threw two of them at an age when most pitchers had already retired. His record-setting fifth no-hitter came with the Astros in 1981. It wasn't until nine seasons later that Ryan threw number 6. He signed with the Rangers in 1989, and in 1990 he no-hit the A's. He was 43 at the time, and a no-hitter had never been thrown by anyone older. At least not until the next May, when Ryan no-hit the Blue Jays at Arlington Stadium. The 1993 season was the 27th and final one for the Ryan Express, and he retired having played the most career seasons in the modern era.

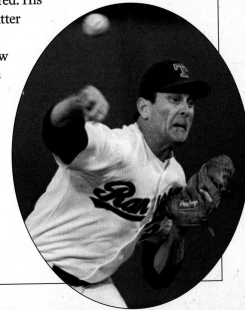

TORONTO BLUE JAYS AL EAST

1977
Expansion franchise awarded to Toronto in 1976

FOUNDED

THE GREATS

Carlos Delgado, First Baseman Delgado had eight straight 30-homer seasons in Toronto from 1997 through 2004, and had six 100-RBI seasons in that span. He's the franchise's all-time leader in both categories.

Roy Halladay, Pitcher The righthander finished in the top five in AL Cy Young voting five times in his 12 seasons with the Jays, including in 2003, when he won the award.

WINS: 2
LOSSES: 0

WORLD SERIES

José Bautista, Outfielder After a slow start to his career, Bautista became one of baseball's best hitters after joining the Jays. He led the majors in home runs in 2010 (54) and 2011 (43).

1992
96–66 regular-season record, World Series champions

BEST SEASON

Dave Stieb, Pitcher Toronto's ace during the 1980s, Stieb made seven All-Star teams and led the AL in ERA (2.48) in 1985.

GOOD TO KNOW

With a 3–2 series lead in the 1993 Fall Classic, Toronto trailed the Phillies 6–5 in Game 6 heading into the bottom of the ninth. Jays speedster Rickey Henderson led off the inning with a walk against Philly closer Mitch Williams. Two batters later, Paul Molitor singled to make it first and second with one out. That's when Joe Carter *(right)* came to the plate. On a 2-and-2 pitch, Carter pulled the ball over the leftfield wall at the SkyDome. He joined Bill Mazeroski (1960, for the Pirates) as the only other player to hit a World Series–winning walk-off home run. As Blue Jays radio announcer Tom Cheek said, "Touch 'em all, Joe, you'll never hit a bigger home run in your life!"

WASHINGTON NATIONALS

NL EAST

1969
Originally Montreal Expos (1969–2004). Became Washington Nationals in 2005

FOUNDED

WORLD SERIES

WINS: 0
LOSSES: 0

BEST SEASON

1994
74–40, MLB's best regular-season record that year (season shortened due to player strike)

THE GREATS

Gary Carter, Catcher One of the best to ever play behind the plate, Carter was a seven-time All-Star for the Expos and led the NL in RBIs in 1984 (106).

Tim Raines, Outfielder Raines, an All-Star in seven of his 13 seasons with Montreal, was one of the most dynamic leadoff hitters in baseball history. He led the NL in stolen bases four straight seasons, from 1981 through 1984.

Andre Dawson, Outfielder Known as the Hawk, Dawson starred for Montreal in the 1970s and 1980s. He had five seasons with at least 20 home runs and 20 stolen bases.

Bryce Harper, Outfielder One of the biggest stars of today's game, Harper earned NL MVP in 2015, when he was just 23 years old.

GOOD TO KNOW

Politics can get tough, but no tougher than the Presidents Race held every game at Nationals Park. The event pits costumed former presidents (with comically large heads) against each other in a race to home plate. There's plenty of pushing, shoving, and tripping along the way. When it began, in 2006, the four presidents on Mount Rushmore raced each other (*from left*: Teddy Roosevelt, Thomas Jefferson, Abraham Lincoln, and George Washington). The big story in the race's early years: Teddy never won. The 26th president lost 525 consecutive races before finally getting a win on the last day of the 2012 regular season, the year the franchise made the playoffs for the first time since moving to D.C. *Bully!*

STADIUM DIMENSIONS

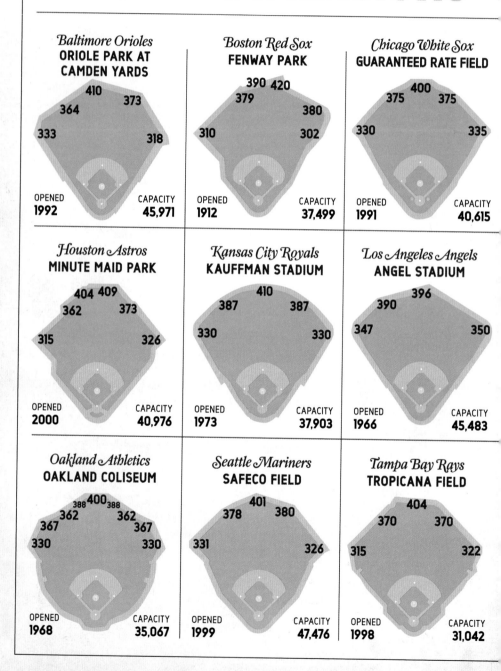

Baltimore Orioles
ORIOLE PARK AT CAMDEN YARDS
410
373
364
333
318
OPENED
1992
CAPACITY
45,971

Boston Red Sox
FENWAY PARK
390 420
379
380
310
302
OPENED
1912
CAPACITY
37,499

Chicago White Sox
GUARANTEED RATE FIELD
400
375
375
330
335
OPENED
1991
CAPACITY
40,615

Houston Astros
MINUTE MAID PARK
404 409
362
373
315
326
OPENED
2000
CAPACITY
40,976

Kansas City Royals
KAUFFMAN STADIUM
410
387
387
330
330
OPENED
1973
CAPACITY
37,903

Los Angeles Angels
ANGEL STADIUM
396
390
347
350
OPENED
1966
CAPACITY
45,483

Oakland Athletics
OAKLAND COLISEUM
388 400 388
362
362
367
367
330
330
OPENED
1968
CAPACITY
35,067

Seattle Mariners
SAFECO FIELD
401
378
380
331
326
OPENED
1999
CAPACITY
47,476

Tampa Bay Rays
TROPICANA FIELD
404
370
370
315
322
OPENED
1998
CAPACITY
31,042

One of the reasons baseball is such a unique sport: The playing field comes in all different sizes. Here's a look at the dimensions (in feet) of the 15 American League ballparks.

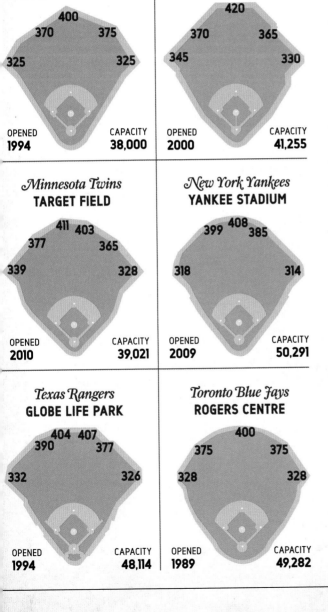

Cleveland Indians
PROGRESSIVE FIELD

400
370   375
325   325

OPENED **1994**   CAPACITY **38,000**

Detroit Tigers
COMERICA PARK

420
370   365
345   330

OPENED **2000**   CAPACITY **41,255**

Minnesota Twins
TARGET FIELD

411   403
377   365
339   328

OPENED **2010**   CAPACITY **39,021**

New York Yankees
YANKEE STADIUM

399   408   385
318   314

OPENED **2009**   CAPACITY **50,291**

Texas Rangers
GLOBE LIFE PARK

404   407
390   377
332   326

OPENED **1994**   CAPACITY **48,114**

Toronto Blue Jays
ROGERS CENTRE

400
375   375
328   328

OPENED **1989**   CAPACITY **49,282**

American League

STADIUM DIMENSIONS

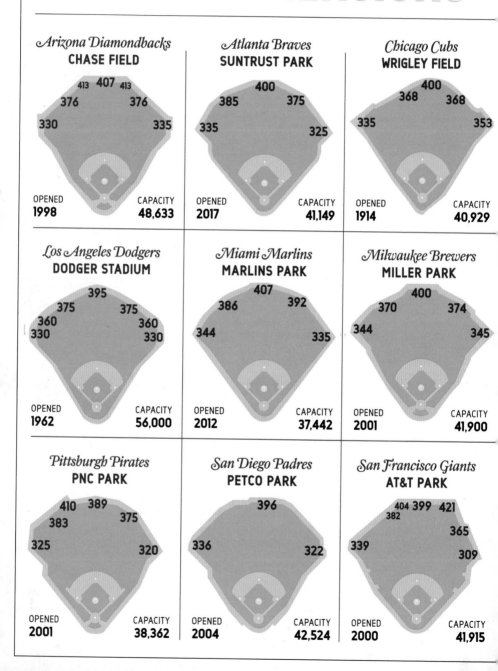

Arizona Diamondbacks
CHASE FIELD

413 407 413
376 376
330 335

OPENED
1998

CAPACITY
48,633

Atlanta Braves
SUNTRUST PARK

400
385 375
335 325

OPENED
2017

CAPACITY
41,149

Chicago Cubs
WRIGLEY FIELD

400
368 368
335 353

OPENED
1914

CAPACITY
40,929

Los Angeles Dodgers
DODGER STADIUM

395
375 375
360 360
330 330

OPENED
1962

CAPACITY
56,000

Miami Marlins
MARLINS PARK

407
386 392
344 335

OPENED
2012

CAPACITY
37,442

Milwaukee Brewers
MILLER PARK

400
370 374
344 345

OPENED
2001

CAPACITY
41,900

Pittsburgh Pirates
PNC PARK

410 389
383 375
325 320

OPENED
2001

CAPACITY
38,362

San Diego Padres
PETCO PARK

396
336 322

OPENED
2004

CAPACITY
42,524

San Francisco Giants
AT&T PARK

404 399 421
382
365
339 309

OPENED
2000

CAPACITY
41,915

...ake a look at the National League's great American ball parks ...
...including Great American Ball Park, home of the Cincinnati Reds,
...and historic Wrigley Field, the NL's oldest stadium.

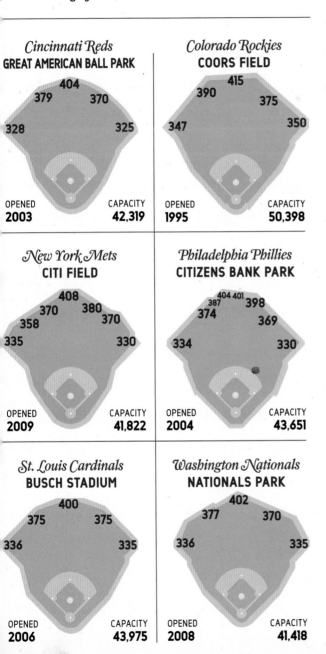

Cincinnati Reds
GREAT AMERICAN BALL PARK

404
379 370
328 325

OPENED	CAPACITY
2003	**42,319**

Colorado Rockies
COORS FIELD

415
390 375
347 350

OPENED	CAPACITY
1995	**50,398**

New York Mets
CITI FIELD

408
370 380
358 370
335 330

OPENED	CAPACITY
2009	**41,822**

Philadelphia Phillies
CITIZENS BANK PARK

404 401
387 398
374 369
334 330

OPENED	CAPACITY
2004	**43,651**

St. Louis Cardinals
BUSCH STADIUM

400
375 375
336 335

OPENED	CAPACITY
2006	**43,975**

Washington Nationals
NATIONALS PARK

402
377 370
336 335

OPENED	CAPACITY
2008	**41,418**

National League

Chapter
7

TALK THE TALK

If you want to be a real baseball
fan, you have to know the lingo.
Or how else will you identify a
submariner as a LOOGY?
Or avoid the Mendoza Line?
We've got you covered.

Around the Horn It's part celebration, part warmup for the defense. After the first or second out of an inning, if the bases are empty, you'll see the infield play a little catch, usually between the third baseman, second baseman, and shortstop. It's unclear exactly where the term came from, but it might have been inspired by North American cross-country travel in the 19th century. Before the Panama Canal was created, ships sailed below the southern tip of South America, Cape Horn, going "around the Horn" to get from the East Coast to the West Coast.

USE IT "The pitcher threw strike three for the first out. The catcher tossed the ball down to third base, and the infielders threw around the horn."

Atom Ball A heartbreaking moment for any hitter. It's an "at 'em" ball, as in a hard hit that becomes an out because it was hit right at a defender.

USE IT "He ripped that pitch directly at the third baseman, who caught it for the third out. The pitcher got out of a tough spot thanks to an atom ball."

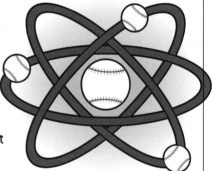

Backdoor Breaking Ball Breaking balls (mostly curveballs and sliders) look as if they're going to be strikes before they move out of the zone. The goal is to entice the hitter to swing at (and, hopefully for the pitcher, miss) a bad pitch. The backdoor breaking ball is the opposite: The pitch looks as if it's going to be outside and/or high, then drops into the strike zone.

USE IT "There's a called strike three! That curveball caught the outside corner of the plate. The batter was fooled by the backdoor breaking ball."

Balk When a pitcher makes any kind of illegal motion to fool a base runner. The play is called dead before the pitch is thrown, and every base runner gets to advance one base.

USE IT "The pitcher was on the rubber and flinched, raising his hands as if he were about to start throwing a pitch. That's a balk, and the runner on second base moves to third."

Baltimore Chop This is an old-school trick from the early 20th century, when baseball was in its Dead Ball era. Due to cavernous ballparks and squishy baseballs, there were few home runs, and teams relied on moving one base at a time. In Baltimore, future Hall of Famer John McGraw and his teammates learned to pound the ball straight down. It would bounce high off home plate or the dirt right in front of the plate (which, in Baltimore, the groundskeeper purposely packed extra hard), allowing the batter to beat out the play at first base. To this day, a lucky, high-hop infield hit off the plate is still known as a Baltimore chop.
USE IT "The hitter didn't make good contact, but he reached anyway with the Baltimore chop. The pitcher had no chance to get the out at first."

Basket Catch In the early days of baseball, when gloves were smaller, this kind of catch was fairly common. Nowadays, most outfielders catch the ball above their shoulders. But every once in a while, you'll see a player make a catch at his belly button or lower, with the palm of his glove facing up.
USE IT "The leftfielder had to run in a long way to get that ball and misjudged it. But he turned his glove and made the basket catch."

Battery This simply refers to the pitcher and catcher combination. The term dates back to the mid-19th century. Writer Henry Chadwick compared the pitching-catching combination to artillery batteries, or groups of weapons, used by the military.
USE IT "When you're talking about the best battery in the game, lefty Madison Bumgarner and MVP catcher Buster Posey are right up at the top."

Beanball When the pitcher intentionally hits a batter with a pitch.
USE IT "The Yankees' star player was hit by a pitch last inning, and now they've retaliated with a beanball of their own."

Bloop A lucky break for a batter, this kind of weak fly ball goes too far for an infielder to catch but not far enough for an outfielder to make a play.
USE IT "The batter was fooled by the pitch and took an awkward swing, but he ended up with a bloop base hit anyway. It dropped right between the second baseman and the rightfielder."

Bonus Baby When a young player signs his first contract with a big league team—whether it's as a drafted player or an international free agent—the signing bonus, the lump sum of money paid when that contract is signed, is a big deal. A youngster who nets a lot of dough earns this label.
USE IT "He came into the league as a bonus baby, getting $2 million when he signed out of his native Venezuela at age 16."

Brushback If there's one thing pitchers hate, it's hitters crowding the plate and smacking pitches on the outside corner. To get players to back off the plate, a pitcher throws this.
USE IT "The fastball was inside, causing the batter to jump out of the way. That brushback pitch will give him something to think about."

Can of Corn It's a high, routine fly ball that should be an easy play for an outfielder. The name was inspired by old-time grocers, who used to get canned goods for customers by using a pole to knock them off the shelf. The clerks would hold out their aprons to catch the cans.
USE IT "The batter got under the ball a little bit and lifted a can of corn to right. The rightfielder settled under it and made a routine catch."

Charge the Mound Getting hit by a pitch hurts, and sometimes the batter will try to inflict similar pain on the pitcher who hit him. The hit batsman runs out toward the pitcher, presumably to start a fight.
USE IT "The fastball hit the batter in the backside, and he didn't like that one bit. He charged the mound, and a bench-clearing brawl ensued."

Chase a Pitch A batter wants to wait until he gets a nice, fat pitch over the middle of the plate. But sometimes he gets fooled and swings at one that is obviously a ball, usually leading to a swing and a miss (or weak contact).
USE IT "The pitcher was ahead in the count 0 and 2 and threw a curveball that dropped into the dirt. The batter chased the pitch and swung over it for strike three."

Check Swing With all the different pitches thrown at different speeds in the big leagues, you can't blame a hitter for getting confused. This is when the batter starts to swing but stops himself just in time, before the motion is determined to be a swing and therefore a strike.
USE IT "The changeup fooled the batter, but he checked his swing. He held back just enough, and now it's ball two."

Choke Up To generate maximum power, a hitter typically positions his hands far down on the bat, near the knob. Sometimes a hitter will sacrifice power for a chance to make contact and will move his hands higher on the bat, giving him a quicker, more controlled swing.
USE IT "With two strikes, the batter choked up on the bat. He had better control and punched the pitch into rightfield for a base hit."

Cleanup Hitter The fourth hitter in the batting order, often a power hitter. The origin is simple: If the first three batters of the game reach base, the fourth hitter has a chance to clean up the bases with a home run.
USE IT "He usually bats third, but today he'll move back a spot in the order and serve as the cleanup hitter."

Closer The relief pitcher who is asked to close the door on a game by pitching the ninth inning of a tight matchup. The closer is often the best reliever on a team's pitching staff.
USE IT "The Red Sox scored two in the top of the ninth to take a one-run lead, and now they'll call on their closer to try to get the final three outs in the bottom of the inning and end this game."

Comebacker Think fast, pitchers! This is when a ball is hit right back toward the mound, where a good defensive hurler will make the play.
USE IT "The pitcher really fields his position well. On that sharply hit comebacker, he was in a good spot to snag the ground ball and make an easy play at first."

Contact Play It's tough enough to advance a runner *to* third base, so managers employ a series of different strategies to get that runner home. On this play, the runner on third is instructed to take off for home as soon as the batter makes contact with the pitch. The goal is to beat a throw to the plate on a ground ball. The risk is that if the batter hits a line drive, it usually leads to an easy double play.

USE IT "The offense had a contact play on. So even though the batter hit a ground ball, the speedster on third scored easily."

Crowd the Plate Hitters want to be able to make solid contact even on pitches that are thrown on the outside corner of the plate. So this is how they do it: by positioning themselves on top of the inside part of home plate. Of course, pitchers aren't big fans of this practice, since hitters can more easily get to offerings thrown on the outside corner.

USE IT "The pitcher threw inside for a ball, but it seems as if he was just trying to get the batter to back away and stop crowding the plate."

Cutoff Man On a ball hit to the outfield, this player doesn't cover a base. Instead, he positions himself between the fielder and a base, for two reasons: 1) The throw might be too long for the outfielder to make, so the cutoff man will catch the ball and fire it the rest of the way to the base; and 2) more important, it gives the defense some options if there are multiple base runners on the move, allowing the fielders to target a different base runner mid-play.

USE IT "The runner from second got a great jump, but the defense was ready! The cutoff man caught the outfielder's throw short of home plate, fired the ball to second, and threw the batter out."

Cycle It's hard enough to get four hits of any kind in a game. This is the rare instance of a batter getting a single, double, triple, *and* home run— in any order—in a single game.

USE IT "He already had a single, a triple, and a home run in this matchup. He hit the ball into the gap and cruised into second base, completing the cycle."

Dead Ball Era This is essentially the period of time before Babe Ruth came along and started slugging all those home runs. Most stadiums had deep outfield walls, and the ball would get increasingly mushy as the game went on. Players rarely swung for the fences, and scores were very low overall, with teams typically combining for three or four runs every game. The era is considered to have lasted until around 1919.
USE IT "It's another pitchers' duel today. The way the Brewers and the Cardinals are struggling to score runs in this early-season cold weather, you'd think they were playing in the Dead Ball era."

Dig Out Most often employed by the first baseman, it's a move a defensive player makes when he has to field a low throw (or low line drive), often grabbing the ball on a short hop.
USE IT "The third baseman rushed the throw and the ball came in low, but the first baseman was able to dig it out and keep his foot on the bag."

Double Play Depth When there's a runner on first base and fewer than two outs, the shortstop and the second baseman will often position themselves to "turn two"—get two outs on a double play. This typically means that they'll stand closer to second base as well as a bit shallower than usual.
USE IT "After the one-out walk, the second baseman and the shortstop played at double play depth in hopes of ending the inning with one pitch."

Double Switch Because of the designated hitter rule in the American League, this managerial tactic is typically used only in the NL. You'll most often see it when a team is making a pitching change and the pitcher's batting spot is due up the next half-inning. The team will substitute a position player at the same time, allowing him to take over that pitcher's spot in the lineup. Then, the new pitcher moves into the replaced position player's spot in the batting order, so the manager

won't have to bring in a pinch hitter for his new pitcher right away.
USE IT "The manager is going to bring in a lefty from the bullpen; he'll also substitute a new leftfielder in a double switch."

Drag Bunt This is when a lefthanded hitter will try to get a base hit by bunting to the right side of the infield. The idea is to create a tough situation for the first baseman and the pitcher (in terms of fielding the ball and covering first base). The batter will often start to run as he lays down the bunt, making it look as if he's dragging the ball.
USE IT "The leadoff man started the game with a perfect drag

bunt. The pitcher and the first baseman both went for the ball, and the batter had no problem getting to first base on a bunt hit."

Drawn In When a defensive player, or players, is positioned pretty far in because either the defense doesn't have a lot of respect for the hitter or because it needs to stop a runner on third from scoring.
USE IT "With the potential game-winning run on third and nobody out, the defense had no choice but to try to get the out at home. Both the infield and the outfield were drawn in."

Eephus This is a trick pitch from baseball's good ol' days. It's when a pitcher winds up like he always does, then delivers a very slow, high-arching pitch in hopes of catching the hitter completely off-guard. Rip Sewell, a pitcher for the Pirates in the 1940s, is credited with inventing it.
USE IT "That was surprising! The pitcher threw an eephus—his curveball clocked in at only 53 miles per hour."

Farm System Where baseball players are grown. It's a major league franchise's minor league organization, not to be confused with some of the independent minor league teams and leagues around the country. The farm systems are made up of the teams—in classes Triple A, Double A, Advanced A, Class A, Class A Short Season, and rookie ball—that funnel players to the 30 big league teams.

USE IT "The Pirates' farm system is particularly strong. Along with the top rookie this season, they have three players in Triple A and two more in Double A who are considered the best prospects in baseball."

Fielder's Choice Any time a defensive player fields a batted ball and is judged to have been able to retire the batter at first but instead attempts to get an out at another base. The batter reaches first but is not credited with a hit, even if all runners are safe on the play.

USE IT "On a routine ground ball, the second baseman threw across the diamond to get the runner at third, and the batter reached on a fielder's choice."

Five-tool Player If you're assessing players, this is perfection, someone who is considered to excel in all five of the following areas: hitting for average, hitting for power, speed, fielding, and throwing.

USE IT "With four hits, including two home runs, a steal, and a number of dazzling defensive plays so far this game, he's proved he's a five-tool player."

Foul Tip Not to be confused with a foul ball. This is a ball that goes directly from the bat and into the catcher's mitt. (It's different from a pop-up.) It's treated the same way as a swing and a miss, and the ball is live in the event of a stolen base attempt.

USE IT "The batter got a piece of the ball on the swing, but the catcher held on to it. The foul tip was strike three, so the inning is over."

Fungo The name might make it sound like a good time, but this is just a ball hit for practice for the defense. (Not that practice isn't fun.) A fungo bat is longer and lighter than a regulation bat, built for hitting a ball that a batter tosses to himself, rather than one thrown by a pitcher. The batter tosses the ball up and smacks grounders or fly balls to fielders, often during pregame warmups.

USE IT "After making two errors yesterday, he was sure to show up early today to field some fungoes and get his confidence back."

Gap Outside the baseball stadium, it's a good place to get a pair of khakis. On the diamond, it's the space between two outfielders.
USE IT "The batter smoked that pitch into the leftfield gap—neither the centerfielder nor the leftfielder had a chance at making the catch."

Golden Sombrero This is a rough day at the office for any batter. In most games, each hitter comes to the plate three, four, or sometimes five times. If he strikes out four times in a game, the hitter is said to earn this very rare, very special, and very embarrassing kind of hat.
USE IT "He's already struck out three times today—one more and he'll earn the infamous golden sombrero."

Gopher Ball The kind of pitch a hitter can really "go for," which might be the origin. Or it could be "go four," as in the number of bases the batter will touch after hitting it. But either way, it's a big, fat pitch that a hitter drives for a home run.
USE IT "You can tell the pitcher is running out of gas—he threw a gopher ball there that was blasted for a solo home run."

Green Light Sometimes you gotta let hitters just . . . hit. The green light is what a great hitter might get on a 3-and-0 or 3-and-1 count. The manager gives him permission to try to crush a pitch rather than just wait for ball four. This can also refer to a swift base runner who might have permission to try to steal a base whenever he sees fit.
USE IT "Considering how hot he's been lately, you have to think that he'll have the green light here, even on a 3-and-0 count."

Hanging Breaking Ball Typically, a breaking ball is supposed to look as if it's going to be in the strike zone before moving out (a curveball dropping into the dirt, or a slider darting left to right or right to left). But sometimes the pitch doesn't break as much as intended and instead drops right into a batter's sweet spot, making for a very hittable pitch.
USE IT "The pitcher got lucky. He threw a hanging breaking ball that was belt high and right over the middle of the plate. The hitter got under it just a little bit, driving it to the warning track, where it was caught."

Hit-and-run O.K., it really should be called a "run-and-hit" because this is when the runners on base take off when the pitcher begins his delivery as if they're trying to steal. But instead of letting the pitch go, the hitter makes contact and puts the ball into play. This not only gives any runner a head start, it can draw a defensive player out of position as he moves to cover the base on a steal attempt.
USE IT "The hit-and-run worked perfectly there: The second baseman moved to cover second base, and the hitter put a ground ball right where the second baseman had been."

Holding the Runner You'll see teams try to do this when a runner is on first (unless he's a particularly slow runner). It's the art of keeping the runner from getting too big a lead off of first. The defensive player will wait at the base in case the pitcher throws over to try to pick the runner off. (The pitcher may make several attempts.) If the pitcher starts to throw a pitch, the defensive player will slide back closer to his usual position.

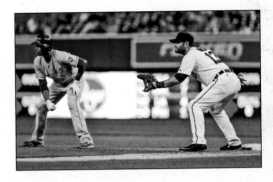

USE IT "The Angels have a four-run lead, but they're going to hold the runner here anyway. That speedster could steal second base easily."

Home Stand Get comfortable. During the regular season, MLB teams typically play the same opponent for a three- or four-game series. This is when two or three of those series are played in a row, at home.
USE IT "The Giants have a lengthy home stand coming up. The team will start this week with a three-game series against the Diamondbacks, then host the Padres for four games and the Rockies for three before heading out on the road."

Hot Stove League Winter rolls around, and there's no baseball to watch. All you can do is gather around the stove to keep warm (well, that's what you had to do in the 19th century when the term was first in circulation) and talk about what to expect next season. The phrase now refers to the trades and free-agent signings that happen every offseason.
USE IT "Once the first big free agent signs, the Hot Stove League always heats up with more signings and plenty of trades."

Immaculate Inning Everyone knows that there are three strikes for each batter and three outs per inning. This is when a pitcher gets through an inning with three consecutive three-pitch strikeouts and only has to throw nine pitches.
USE IT "Fewer than 100 pitchers have ever thrown an immaculate inning, so it was quite a feat when he struck out all three hitters he faced on three pitches each."

Infield Fly Rule Picture this: There are runners on first and second, or the bases are loaded, with fewer than two outs. The batter hits a routine infield pop-up. The runners all have to stay at or very close to their bases, otherwise they'd risk getting doubled off after the infielder catches the ball. But it would be very easy for that infielder to let the ball drop in front of him, then get a quick double play with two force outs, considering no one would be running. This rule is designed to keep that from happening. If the umpire judges the ball to be a routine infield pop-up, he will announce that the batter is out even though the ball is still in mid-air (and he's still out, even if the infielder drops the ball). That keeps the base runners from being forced to run to the next base.
USE IT "With the bases loaded and one out, the batter hit a high pop-up that looked as if it would land around the pitcher's mound. The umpire invoked the infield fly rule, *aaaand* . . . the second baseman made the catch."

Inside–out Swing This is a rather funky-looking approach some hitters take to attacking a pitch. The hitter swings with his hands crossing the plate well before the head of his bat. It often leads to opposite-field hits. Yankees star Derek Jeter *(right)* frequently used this type of swing.
USE IT "It looked a little bit awkward, but the inside-out swing allowed the batter to drive that pitch for a hit to the opposite field. You can see on the replay how his hands came across the plate first."

Junkballer You might sometimes hear this kind of pitcher referred to as "crafty." Some pitchers don't have a great fastball, so they rely on a series of breaking balls and off-speed pitches to try to keep hitters off-balance.
USE IT "This lefty is a classic junkballer. About 80% of his pitches are slow breaking balls."

Launching Pad Heaven for hitters. This is any ballpark that lends itself to lots of home runs, whether it has outfield fences that are closer than usual to home plate or wind patterns that blow out and can carry the ball over the wall.

USE IT "When you're pitching in a launching pad like this, you have to keep the ball low and try to get ground ball outs. Even routine fly balls can get caught in the wind."

Long Reliever No, you do not have to be seven feet tall to pitch long relief. Most relievers only throw one inning at a time. This is a pitcher who doesn't start the game but usually comes in from the bullpen early on and is asked to throw multiple innings.

USE IT "He has settled into his role as a long reliever, and he'll have to step in again tonight. The starting pitcher was pulled after giving up six runs in three innings; this guy will have to pitch three or four innings."

LOOGY This is an abbreviation for a lefthanded specialist: Lefty One Out Guy. Most pitchers are righties. And, typically, lefthanded batters hit better against righthanded pitchers (and righty batters hit lefty pitchers better) because they are able to see the ball earlier. Thus, there are a lot of lefthanded relief pitchers whose only role is to come in and face one lefthanded batter, then come out if the next batter is a righty.

USE IT "This is a big spot here, and the manager will go to the bullpen to summon a LOOGY to face this lefthanded power hitter. A righty is on deck, so the pitcher will probably only face one batter tonight."

Loud Out When the crowd reacts boisterously to the ball jumping off the bat—but it just doesn't end up being a hit, possibly because of a great catch in the outfield (or maybe it was an atom ball, *page 166*). So this term is literal.

USE IT "That ball got crushed, but the centerfielder got back to the wall and made a sensational leaping catch. It's a loud out, but an out nonetheless."

Manufacturing Runs You can't always rely on hitting a bunch of home runs to win a game, especially when facing a great pitcher. Sometimes teams have to scratch and claw to get a runner across the plate. This is the art of using small-ball tactics, such as aggressive baserunning and bunting, in order to turn one measly base hit into a precious run.

USE IT "The Rangers manufactured a run right there. The batter led off the inning with an infield single, stole second, moved to third on a sacrifice bunt, and then scored on a sac fly."

Meat of the Order This is typically the greatest strength of any lineup: the third, fourth, and fifth hitters. These are traditionally the guys who can get on base and hit for power.

USE IT "The Nationals had a tough time getting hits tonight, but the good news is that the meat of the order is due up next inning."

Mendoza Line Mario Mendoza was actually a pretty good player, a slick-fielding shortstop in the 1970s and early 1980s who played for the Pirates, Mariners, and Rangers. But he wasn't much of a hitter, and his batting average seemed to always be hovering around .200. So teammates joked that hitting .200 was the imaginary Mendoza line. And when longtime ESPN broadcaster Chris Berman caught wind of it, the term worked its way into the mainstream.

USE IT "He's been slumping badly; after going 0 for 4 tonight, he's in danger of falling below the Mendoza line."

Mop Up The kind of pitcher who will enter the game when it's already out of reach. In a lopsided matchup, a manager will often send one of his worst relief pitchers to the mound rather than tire out a more valuable arm.

USE IT "The young hurler has struggled this year, and the manager doesn't trust him in close games. You'll probably only see him in a mop-up role if he pitches tonight."

No–decision Whoever is on the mound when the lead is taken for the final time in the game usually gets the win or the loss. A no-decision is what happens if a pitcher either leaves the game when it's tied or leaves a game that later becomes tied or sees a lead change. He doesn't get a win or a loss on his record.

USE IT "The Mets will bring in a new pitcher for the eighth inning of this scoreless game. So despite seven shutout innings from the starter, he'll get a no-decision today."

Opposite Field The side of the field opposite from where a batter would naturally pull the ball. For a righthanded hitter, it's the right side of the field. For a lefthanded hitter, it's the left side. Typically, a batter hits with less power to the opposite field.

USE IT "The pitch was outside, but the righthanded batter reached out and slapped a hit to the opposite field that fell in front of the rightfielder."

Out Pitch Quite literally, this is the throw a pitcher relies on to get an out, usually a strikeout. Essentially, it's his best pitch.

USE IT "Whenever this pitcher gets two strikes on a hitter, you can bet that he's going to throw his out pitch—a nasty curveball. "

Paint the Corner This is what you'll see the best pitchers in baseball doing. It's the art of throwing pitches on the edges of the strike zone (either the inside or the outside part of the plate).

USE IT "It's been a tough day for hitters. This pitcher has been painting the corners with a 95-mile-per-hour fastball, and they just don't know whether or not to swing."

Passed Ball This is similar to a wild pitch, but the blame for the mistake is placed on the catcher instead of the pitcher. A passed ball occurs when a catcher is unable to control a pitch he ordinarily would have been expected to handle, allowing a base runner to advance.
USE IT "The pitch was a belt-high fastball that was just outside. The catcher reacted late, though, and it was a passed ball, allowing the runner on second to move up to third."

Payoff Pitch A pitch thrown when the count is full (three balls and two strikes). The plate appearance might continue if the batter hits a foul ball. But aside from that, the pitch will either result in a strikeout, a walk, or the ball will be put in play.
USE IT "With two outs and a full count, the runner on first will take off. Here's the payoff pitch. . . ."

Pepper It's an old-school game, and a lot of ballparks actually hang NO PEPPER signs to remind players that they're not supposed to play it for fear of an errant ball flying into the crowd. The game consists of a number of fielders crowding  around one player with a bat. The batter hits the ball at a fielder, who then must field it cleanly and throw it back to the batter to hit it to the next fielder. It can be a simple warmup drill, or it can be played competitively, with the batter "out" (and becoming a fielder) if he misses on a swing. A fielder is knocked out for missing a ball or unleashing a wild throw.
USE IT "Some infielders credit their quick hands to playing pepper when they were young."

Phantom Tag Less of a mystery, and more of a simple mistake by an umpire. This is when a fielder doesn't tag a runner, but whether because of a bad angle or a good acting job by the defensive player, the ump calls the runner out anyway.

USE IT "The defense got away with one there. That was a phantom tag on the stolen base attempt—the shortstop clearly didn't reach back far enough to touch the runner."

Pickle A situation in which a base runner doesn't want to find himself. It occurs when a runner is caught between two bases in a rundown. The defensive players will throw back and forth until they close in and tag the runner out.

USE IT "The batter thought he could turn that single into a double, but he would have been thrown out by 15 feet even if he had kept going. Instead, he stopped halfway and was caught in a pickle between first and second."

Pitch Around A strategy used when the defense fears a particular hitter. It's not an intentional walk, but the pitcher throws outside the strike zone to see if he can get the batter to swing at a bad pitch. Typically, this results in a walk.

USE IT "The Marlins are not going to intentionally walk him here. But he already has two home runs today and has been red-hot of late, so they're probably going to pitch around him."

Pitch to Contact An advanced strategy for a pitcher, whose basic job is to throw strikes. This is the art of throwing pitches that the batter will hit, but hit weakly. Why not just go for the strikeout? Because a pitcher can save his arm and pitch deeper into the game if he pitches to contact early in the count, rather than throwing the usually four, five, or more pitches it takes to finish off a hitter with a strikeout.

USE IT "Now that he's learned to pitch to contact effectively, he's not striking out as many hitters, but he should be able to throw more innings."

Pitchout Something of a desperate move by the defensive team. In an attempt to throw out a base runner trying to steal, a manager will sometimes call for his pitcher to throw a ball high and outside, allowing his catcher to already be out of his stance when the pitch comes in. He is then in position to make the throw to second much quicker.

USE IT "On a 1-and-2 count with two outs, the Braves went with the pitchout to try to catch a stolen base attempt. The runner wasn't going, though, so it's simply ball two."

Plate Appearance One of the most basic statistics in baseball. A batter gets a plate appearance any time he comes up to hit. The only exception is if an out is made, such as a player caught stealing, for the third out of an inning while the batter is still at the plate. This stat is not to be confused with at bats, which are plate appearances minus walks, hit-by-pitch, sacrifice bunts, and sacrifice flies. When determining league leaders such as the batting title, plate appearances—not at bats—are used to determine whether or not a hitter played enough to win the statistical title. (For instance, to win a batting title, you have to average more than 3.1 plate appearances over a season, which is 162 games most years.)

USE IT "He's had four plate appearances today, but it's been three walks and a hit-by-pitch, so he doesn't have an official at bat yet."

Platoon Because lefthanded batters typically hit better against righthanded pitchers, and righthanded batters are usually better against lefty pitchers, managers will often have two players share an everyday spot in the lineup. The game's starter is determined by whether there's a righty or a lefty pitching for the opponent.

USE IT "The lefty slugger used to start every game, but since he's really struggled against lefthanders this year, the manager is using him in a platoon situation."

Player to Be Named Later No one in baseball history has been traded more often. Teams sometimes agree to a trade in which one team knows the player it wants, but the other team wants or needs more time to decide what it wants in return. So part of the trade is announced as a PTBNL, and the teams have six months to figure out how to complete the trade. Sometimes it ends with a cash payment instead of an actual player. And yes, four times in baseball history, the PTBNL has been the player in the other half of the deal. In other words, a player was traded for himself!
USE IT "The Cubs traded for a lefthanded reliever, but it's not clear what they'll give up—right now it's a player to be named later."

Power Alley The areas in left centerfield and right centerfield, named because that's where you typically see the longest hits go. In other words, it's the area where the ball goes when power hitters get hold of a pitch.
USE IT "The batter was looking for a fastball and crushed it over the fence in the leftfield power alley. All the centerfielder and leftfielder could do was turn and watch."

Productive Out It's never as good as actually reaching base safely, but this is the result of a play in which the batter is retired, but another base runner is able to advance.
USE IT "The batter was disappointed, but it was a productive out. The runner on second moved to third on the groundout."

Quality Start In a way, this stat is the most basic goal for a starting pitcher: six or more innings pitched, and three or fewer earned runs allowed. A pitcher can be credited with a quality start in a loss, even if he is named the losing pitcher.
USE IT "The pitcher hasn't been particularly sharp today: He gave up five runs over six innings before exiting the game. But only three of those were earned runs, so he'll get credited with a quality start."

Quick Pitch Baseball is a game of rhythm, and typically the pitcher wants to get the ball back and fire the next pitch, while the hitter might be interested in doing little things to upset that timing (such as step out of the batter's box and adjust his helmet and batting gloves). The batter isn't supposed to waste time, but he also isn't supposed to be caught off-guard. If the umpire rules that the pitcher threw too soon in an attempt to deceive the hitter, the ump can rule it a quick pitch, which is an automatic ball and also a balk if there are any runners on base.

USE IT "It seems the pitcher worked a little too fast right there. The batter was not ready, and the umpire ruled it a quick pitch. Ball three!"

Sacrifice Bunt
Sometimes a hitter will bunt to try to get on base. But this is when a batter lays down a bunt to get the ball in play and allow a teammate on base to advance. The batter knows he will likely be thrown out at first base. It's a strategy used much less in the modern game as advanced statistics have shown it is unwise to give up an out unless a hitter is hopelessly overmatched.

USE IT "With a man on first and one out, the pitcher comes to the plate. He's hitting just .053 this season, so we'll likely see a sacrifice bunt attempt."

Scoring Position Runners on second or third base are considered to be in scoring position—they have a good chance to make it home on any base hit that reaches the outfield.

USE IT "He's been an RBI machine, and he now has a big opportunity with two runners in scoring position. The runner on second is speedy, so a hit would almost certainly score two runs."

Shagging It's the routine of jogging around the outfield during batting practice and catching fly balls, then tossing them back to the infield.

Many teams used to ask pitchers to do it, though in the modern game it's usually a mix of pitchers, batboys, and other staffers. It's mostly a harmless exercise, though there have been a handful of injuries resulting from shagging fly balls over the years. Most recently, All-Star closer Mariano Rivera suffered a season-ending knee injury in May 2012. Rivera returned a year later and resumed the practice of shagging flies before games.

USE IT "Batting practice always goes a little more smoothly if the balls get returned quickly. So it helps to have as many people shagging flies in the outfield as possible."

Shake Off When the catcher signals for a certain pitch but the pitcher wants to throw something different, how does the pitcher communicate that? With a simple head shake to say, "No."

USE IT "The pitcher looked in for the sign from his catcher and shook it off, so the catcher gave him a new pitch."

Shelled In military terminology, if a target is under heavy fire from artillery, it is said to be getting shelled. The same thing is said for pitchers who are giving up hit after hit.

USE IT "The lefty didn't have his best stuff today, and you could tell. He got shelled out there, giving up 10 hits in two innings."

Shoestring Catch A tough grab for an outfielder, when he's running in to get the ball and makes the grab just before it hits the ground. You know, about even with his shoelaces.
USE IT "On a sharp line drive, the centerfielder came in and made the shoestring catch, snagging the ball just before it hit the ground."

Sit on a Pitch A big part of hitting is anticipating what kind of pitch is coming—if you're expecting a fastball and get a changeup, your timing is going to be way off and you're probably going to swing and miss. If you sit on a pitch, you have decided, before the pitcher delivers, that you will only swing if he throws a particular kind of pitch.
USE IT "He said after the game that he was sitting on a pitch, expecting a fastball all the way, and when he got it, he hammered it well over the rightfield wall."

Small Ball Most teams rely on "a bloop and a blast" type of strategy to score runs, basically waiting for a home run to clear the bases. But there are still a few teams, short on power hitters, who generate their offense the old-fashioned way: aggressive hitting and baserunning, and a reliance on productive outs *(page 185)* to move runners along.
USE IT "You'll see the Padres play a lot of small ball this year. The players won't hit many home runs, but they will use their speed to put pressure on opposing defenses and pitchers."

Squeeze Play Sometimes you have to get creative to score a run from third base. A bunt seems a strange way to get a runner home, when you consider that a bunt lands close to home plate, seemingly making it easier to throw out a runner headed for home. But managers sometimes try to catch an opponent off-guard with a squeeze play. There's the safety squeeze, in which the runner on third will take a cautious approach, waiting until the bunt has been laid down to break for home. And there's a suicide squeeze, in which the runner breaks for home on the pitch, essentially a stolen base attempt of home if the batter misses on the bunt.

USE IT "Considering how badly that hitter had been slumping, it wasn't too much of a surprise that the Astros used a squeeze play there. The batter laid down a perfect bunt, allowing the runner on third to beat the throw home."

Stretch

Have you ever noticed that when there are runners on base, pitchers rarely use a full windup? If they did, base runners would steal second and third easily. So the solution is throwing from the stretch: The pitcher starts standing sideways, and his motion involves only a kick-step forward. Many relief pitchers throw exclusively from the stretch, since they're often summoned to the game when there are already runners on base. Most pitchers are more comfortable throwing out of the windup, but some prefer the simplicity of the stretch.

USE IT "That's the first man the Reds have had on base all game, so the pitcher will throw from the stretch for the first time."

Submariner

A pitcher who ends up releasing the ball from below his belt. The style requires an unusual delivery that often causes confusion for hitters, especially the first time they see it in a game.

USE IT "The righthanded submariner is especially tough on righthanded hitters. The ball is released

so low that it looks as if it's coming out of the ground, making it hard for the hitter to see."

Take This term often causes confusion among baseball beginners, but it's *not* when you take a swing at a pitch. It's when you watch a pitch go by.
USE IT "The count is now 3 and 0, and the pitcher is in danger of walking his fourth consecutive hitter. You have to think the batter will take this next pitch no matter what and make the pitcher throw a strike."

Unearned Run As far as wins and losses go, a run is a run. But as far as a pitcher's statistics go, runs can be earned—or unearned, if the official scorer determines that the run only scored because of an error or a passed ball. An unearned run does not count against a pitcher's ERA (earned run average).
USE IT "That ball went right through the shortstop's legs, allowing the go-ahead run to score with two outs. It was an unearned run, but it was still a devastating play for the pitcher."

Vulture In most games, the winning pitcher ends up being the starting pitcher. But sometimes a win is "vultured" when a short reliever comes into a game and happens to be the pitcher of record when there's a lead change. In some especially infuriating situations, that relief pitcher actually blows a lead, but then picks up a win when his team retakes the lead.
USE IT "The closer blew the save, but he ended up a vulture tonight, picking up the win after the Diamondbacks retook the lead in the bottom of the ninth."

Walk-off Time to celebrate! This is any play that wins the game for the hitting team in the bottom of the last inning. There are walk-off home runs, walk-off singles, walk-off walks. There have even been walk-off balks. The name comes from the fact that after the play is over, you can stroll off the field because the game just ended.
USE IT "That's as dramatic as it gets. The Tigers came back to tie it in the bottom of the eighth, then won it one inning later on a walk-off home run."

Wheelhouse The sweet spot for a hitter. Most of the time, this is a pitch that is belt high, over the middle of the plate. But some hitters like pitches in other spots—for instance, a lot of lefthanders like pitches that are low and inside.
USE IT "The pitch was supposed to be low and outside, but he left it over the middle of the plate, right in the hitter's wheelhouse. The pitcher knew it was going out of the park as soon as contact was made."

Wheel Play The defense sometimes sets this into motion when there's a runner on second and the batter is expected to bunt. The third baseman charges toward home plate to field the ball, while the shortstop vacates his usual spot on the diamond and sprints over to cover third base. The players moving at the same time in the same direction resemble a wheel turning.
USE IT "The defense played it aggressively on the sacrifice bunt, putting on the wheel play to try to get the out at third base, but the runner slid into third before the shortstop could get the tag down."

Work the Count This takes patience on the part of the hitter. Instead of attacking early in a plate appearance, the hitter makes the pitcher throw a lot of pitches, resulting in a long at bat.
USE IT "After fouling off a couple of two-strike pitches, the hitter took ball three. He has really worked the count this at bat."

PHOTO CREDITS

INTRODUCTION Frank Jansky/Icon Sportswire/Getty Images (Lindor); Bob Levey/Getty Images (Astros fans); Billie Weiss/Boston Red Sox/Getty Images (field)

KNOW THESE NUMBERS Bettmann/Getty Images (opener, Aaron career home runs, Oh, Ruth, Cobb, DiMaggio); Jed Jacobsohn/Getty Images (Bonds career); Mark Rucker/Transcendental Graphics/Getty Images (Gibson, Keefe, Radbourn); Archive Photos/Getty Images (Maris); Sporting News/Getty Images (Bonds single-season, Berra, Clemens); Jim McIsaac/Getty Images (Alex Rodriguez); Kyodo/AP (Martinez); Otto Greule Jr./Allsport/Getty Images (Moyer); Wally McNamee/Corbis/Getty Images (Rose); Dan Levine/AFP/Getty Images (Ichiro); Sporting News and Rogers Photo Archive/Getty Images (Burnett); Corbis/Getty Images (Duffy); Walter Iooss Jr. (Ripken); Allsport/Getty Images (Griffey); Focus on Sport/Getty Images (Mattingly, Gibson, Jackson); Hy Peskin/Getty Images (Long); National Baseball Hall of Fame Library/MLB Photos/Getty Images (Young); Underwood Archives/Getty Images (Johnson); Harry How/ALLSPORT/Getty Images (Rivera); Lisa Blumenfeld/Getty Images (Francisco Rodriguez); Jonathan Daniel/Getty Images (Ryan); Anthony J. Causi/Icon SMI/Corbis/Getty Images (Yankees); ho/AP (Cubs); Craig Lassig/AFP/Getty Images (Mariners); Tony Triolo (Aaron field view, most career RBIs); Neil Leifer (Aaron close-up, most career RBIs); Stanley Weston/Getty Images (Wilson); Brian Bahr/AFP/Getty Images (Henderson sliding); Heinz Kluetmeier (Henderson running); G Fiume/Getty Images (Reynolds); Christian Petersen/Getty Images (Chapman)

OBSCURE FACTS Getty Images (laundry basket, top hat, red socks, white socks, shoe, glove, handshake, earthquake, closed sign, watch, Veeck); Michael Zagaris/Oakland Athletics/Getty Images (Venditte, 2); Bettmann/Getty Images (Chilcott, mail, Mack, Nuxhall, Pirates, Young, Piersall); Jim Gund (Taylor); Chuck Solomon (Jeter); iStockphoto/Getty Images (sky); Focus on Sport/Getty Images (Youngblood, 2; Griffeys; Perry brothers); Denis Poroy/Getty Images (Colon); Vincent Ethier/MLB Photos/Getty Images (box of balls); Tim Clayton/Corbis/Getty Images (ball); Stan Grossfeld/The Boston Globe/Getty Images (mud); Diamond Images/Getty Images (sheet music, fireworks); Pouya Dianat/Atlanta Braves/Getty Images (grass); Bruce Bennett Studios/Getty Images (Paige); Donald Miralle/Allsport/Getty Images (Tatis); Mark Rucker/Transcendental Graphics/Getty Images (Taft, Spiders); Adam Glanzman/Getty Images (Ortiz); Photo Reproduction by Transcendental Graphics/Getty Images (Gaedel); Manny Millan (shorts); MLB Photos/Getty Images (Doby); John Soohoo/MLB Photos/Getty Images (Caray); Maddie Meyer/Getty Images (names on jerseys); Phil Velasquez/Chicago Tribune/MCT/Getty Images (ivy); AP (Alou brothers); Bob Rosato (Pujols); Sean M. Haffey/Getty Images (Trout); Tony Quinn/Icon Sportswire/Getty Images (Harper); Adam Hunger/Getty Images (Judge); eBay (Aaron card); Mitchell Layton/Getty Images (Santiago, Rauch); Ronald C. Modra/Sports Imagery/Getty Images (Expos)

SKILLS TO MASTER Matt Brown/Angels Baseball LP/Getty Images (get an autograph); Hannah Foslien/Getty Images (freeze frame); Mark Goldman/Icon SMI/Corbis/Getty Images (block); Mike McGinnis/Getty Images (rise and fire); Sean M. Haffey/Getty Images (get a ball); Steve Russell/Toronto Star/Getty Images (fan resting); Elsa/Getty Images (get on camera); Erick W. Rasco (plain hot dog); Levy Restaurants (Dodgers); Aramark (Royals, Pirates); courtesy of Chicago White Sox/Jordan Doyle (White Sox); Photo Illustration by Sarah Sachs/Arizona Diamondbacks/Getty Images (Diamondbacks);

Matthew Pearce/Icon Sportswire/Getty Images (Rangers)

RUN A TEAM Jonathan Daniel/Getty Images (Ricketts and Epstein); Brad Krause/Four Seam Images/AP (Iowa Cubs); Ronald Martinez/Getty Images (Correa); Bob Levey/Getty Images (Verlander); LG Patterson/MLB Photos/Getty Images (Reddick, 2); Harry How/Getty Images (Altuve); G Fiume/Getty Images (Showalter); Chris Williams/Icon Sportswire/Getty Images (setting the lineup); Amazon Statcast (defensive positioning); Nick Wosika/Icon Sportswire/Getty Images (bullpen use); Victor Decolongon/Getty Images (Trout); Jason Miller/Getty Images (Kluber); Stephen Dunn/Getty Images (Simmons); Kyle Emery/Icon Sportswire/Getty Images (Neshek); Mitchell Layton/Getty Images (Santana)

HE REMINDS ME OF Ronald Martinez/Getty Images (Verlander opener); Rich Pilling/MLB Photos/Getty Images (Ryan opener, Rivera); Jason O. Watson/Getty Images (Trout); Louis Requena/MLB Photos/Getty Images (Mantle, Gibson); Ezra Shaw/Getty Images (Kershaw); Focus on Sport/Getty Images (Koufax, Morgan, Robinson); Brace Hemmelgarn/Minnesota Twins/Getty Images (Altuve); Jamie Sabau/Getty Images (Scherzer); Maddie Meyer/Getty Images (Sale); Rex Brown/WireImage/Getty Images (Johnson); John Cordes/Icon Sportswire/Getty Images (Simmons); St. Louis Cardinals Archive/Getty Images (Smith); Dustin Bradford/Getty Images (Posey); Bettmann/Getty Images (Berra, Greenberg, Mize); Frank Jansky/Icon Sportswire/Getty Images (Jansen); G Fiume/Getty Images (Harper); Mitchell Layton/Getty Images (Griffey); Christian Petersen/Getty Images (Stanton); Michael Hickey/Getty Images (Bryant); Mickey Pfleger (Schmidt); Duane Burleson/Getty Images (Cabrera); Joe Robbins/Getty Images (Votto)

TEAM TIDBITS Mark Rucker/Transcendental Graphics/Getty Images (Ruth on opener); Keith Torrie/NY Daily News Archive/Getty Images (Diamondbacks); Kathy Willens/AP (Braves); Focus on Sport/Getty Images (Orioles, Reds, Tigers, Astros, Brewers, Pirates); Buyenlarge/Getty Images (Red Sox); Paul Beaty/AP (Cubs); The Stanley Weston Archive/Getty Images (White Sox); Brace Hemmelgarn/Minnesota Twins/Getty Images (Indians); Glenn Asakawa/The Denver Post (Rockies); Sporting News/Getty Images (Royals, Phillies); Josh Barber/Angels Baseball LP/Getty Images (Angels); Bettmann/Getty Images (Dodgers); Jamie Squire/Getty Images (Marlins); Rick Stewart/Getty Images (Twins); NY Daily News Archive/Getty Images (Mets); Louis Van Oeyen/Western Reserve Historical Society/Getty Images (Yankees); Courtesy of Sony Pictures (A's); AP (Cardinals); Denis Poroy/Getty Images (Padres); Frank Hurley/NY Daily News Archive/Getty Images (Giants); Otto Greule Jr/Getty Images (Mariners); J. Meric/Getty Images (Rays); Bill Janscha/AP (Rangers); MLB Photos/Getty Images (Blue Jays); Mitchell Layton/Getty Images (Nationals)

TALK THE TALK Thearon W. Henderson/Getty Images (basket catch); Chris LaFrance/Icon Sportswire/Getty Images (beanball); Justin Edmonds/Getty Images (choke up); Michael Zagaris/Oakland Athletics/Getty Images (drag bunt, fungo); Dave Reginek/Getty Images (holding the runner); Brad Mangin/MLB Photos/Getty Images (infield fly rule); Ezra Shaw/Getty Images (inside-out swing); AP (Mendoza line); Bettmann/Getty Images (pepper); Rob Tringali/Sportschrome/Getty Images (pickle); Mike Stobe/Getty Images (plate appearance); Stephen Brashear/Getty Images (sacrifice bunt); Mark Cunningham/MLB Photos/Getty Images (shake off, walk-off); Rich Pilling/MLB Photos/Getty Images (submariner)

BACK COVER Hy Peskin/Getty Images (DiMaggio); Getty Images (glove)